Crucible for Change

Engaging Impasse through Communal Contemplation and Dialogue

Edited by
Nancy Sylvester, IHM and Mary Jo Klick

SOR JUANA PRESS

San Antonio, Texas

Published by Sor Juana Press
Co-Editors: Elise D. García and Carol Coston, OP

Design by Susan E. Klein of Sister Creek Studios, San Antonio, Texas. (www.sistercreekstudios.com)

Printed by Crumrine Printers, Inc., San Antonio, Texas, a family-owned union shop. ⬤◖◗◖◗ " (www.crumrine.com)

♻ The materials used in the production of this book reflect our ecological concerns. It is printed with soy inks on 100% post-consumer recycled paper, processed chlorine-free, supplied by Dolphin Blue, a Dallas, Texas-based company specializing in environmentally responsible office products. (www.dolphinblue.com)

ISBN 0-9740243-9-2

Sor Juana Press
28 Hein Road
Boerne, Texas 78006
www.santuariosisterfarm.org
or www.sisterfarm.org

ABOUT SOR JUANA PRESS

Sor Juana Press is a project of Santuario Sisterfarm, a nonprofit organization rooted in the Texas Hill Country and grounded in the rich multicultural legacy of the Borderlands. Founded in 2002, Santuario Sisterfarm inspirits the work of transforming human relationships with Earth and among other humans by moving from dominance to co-creative partnerships, drawing on insights from wisdom traditions, nature, the new science, and women's ways. Santuario Sisterfarm advances its mission by cultivating diversity—biodiversity and cultural diversity.

Sor Juana Press is dedicated to publishing the works of women—particularly women of color and women religious—on topics rooted in women's spirituality and relationship with Earth, *la Tierra, nuestra madre*.

The Press invokes the name and honors the memory of Sor Juana Inés de la Cruz (1648-1695), a Mexican nun, scholar, poet, playwright, musician, and scientist—a woman with a *sed de conocer* (thirst for knowing)—who was silenced for advocating women's education. She is the first writer in the Americas to speak out in favor of a woman's right to learn and express concern about human depredation of the environment.

Other Books by Sor Juana Press

EARTH SPIRITUALITY: IN THE CATHOLIC AND DOMINICAN TRADITIONS by Sharon Therese Zayac, O.P., *Dominican Women on Earth* Series (Issue No. 1, June 2003).

PERMACULTURE: FINDING OUR OWN VINES AND FIG TREES by Carol Coston, O.P., *Dominican Women on Earth* Series (Issue No. 2, August 2003).

EARTH, OUR HOME: BIBLICAL WITNESS IN THE HEBREW SCRIPTURES by Sarah Ann Sharkey, O.P., *Dominican Women on Earth* Series (Issue No. 3, February 2004).

ENCOUNTERING MYSTERY IN THE WILDERNESS: ONE WOMAN'S VISION QUEST by Margaret Galiardi, O.P., *Dominican Women on Earth* Series (Issue No. 4, April 2004).

To Constance FitzGerald, OCD, whose seminal work on impasse and the dark night of the soul continues to inspire so many of us,

and to all who in their search for transformation are willing to engage the impasse and awaken their imaginations to new ways of being and acting.

Contents

Acknowledgments. viii

Everything Before Us Brought Us to This Moment:
Introduction and Context. 1
by Nancy Sylvester, IHM

Being Present to a Process:
Designing Circles of Communal Contemplation and Dialogue 19
by Mary McCann, IHM

One Inch Long, Many Miles Deep:
A Preacher Mines Ecclesial Impasse 37
by Patricia Bruno, OP

Becoming the Change We Want To See:
A Leadership Team Discerns New Ways of Exercising Power 51
by Joellen McCarthy, BVM; Peggy Nolan, BVM;
and Mary Ann Zollmann, BVM

Resisting the Isolating Allure of Impasse:
*A Lawyer, Lobbyist, and Poet Risks Moving
Into Uncharted Territory* 67
by Simone Campbell, SSS

Be-ing in the Story:
*A Conversation Reflecting on Impasse
through the Lens of the New Cosmology* 81
by Margaret Galiardi, OP and Rose Mary Meyer, BVM

Embracing Impasse and Her Sisters:
*A Feminist Liberationist Theologian Comes To Live
Confidently with Uncertainty*. 97
by Mary Hunt

Communal Quest Makes the Difference:
A Congregation Leader Finds New Ways
To Speak Truth with Love. 109
by Pat Kozak, CSJ

A New Energy, A New Hope:
A Spiritual Director Releases the Oppressive Hold of Impasse. 123
by Elinor Shea, OSU

The Horizon Just Before Dawn:
A Dark Place of Promise
for a Grieving Human Rights Activist. 139
by Margaret Swedish

Reflection Questions on CRUCIBLE FOR CHANGE. 150

Endnotes. 154

About the Editors. 158

Institute for Communal Contemplation
and Dialogue. 160

Acknowledgments

CRUCIBLE FOR CHANGE would not exist were it not for the courage and grace of seventy-two women, who participated in the yearlong project we called, *Engaging Impasse: Circles of Contemplation and Dialogue.* Their willingness to risk entering a process that invited them to share their experiences of impasse and power-lessness was remarkable. It testifies to the great yearning in us to search together, from a faith perspective, to find meaning in the midst of shifting worldviews.

I especially thank the twelve women who were willing to put their experiences of the circle gatherings in writing, in the stories that make up this book: Patricia Bruno, OP; Simone Campbell, SSS; Margaret Galiardi, OP; Mary Hunt; Pat Kozak, CSJ; Mary McCann, IHM; Joellen McCarthy, BVM; Rose Mary Meyer, BVM; Peggy Nolan, BVM; Elinor Shea, OSU; Margaret Swedish; and Mary Ann Zollmann, BVM.

It took a communal effort to create the *Engaging Impasse* project. The circle gatherings would not have taken place without a group of women who helped transform an insight I had, about engaging impasse communally and contemplatively, into a rich and powerful process. I am deeply grateful to ...

... Design Team members Jean Alvarez, Nancy Conway, CSJ, and Marcia Allen, CSJ for their wisdom, humor, and incredible process and spiritual-direction skills. Their willingness to make room on their full calendars to work with the circles was key to making the project happen.

... Bette Moslander, CSJ for her ongoing support over many years and her willingness to help in the initial design. Dorothy Ettling, CCVI for her deep belief that the gatherings would hold insights for a broader learning community. Doris Klein, CSA for designing the *Engaging Impasse* logo and creating the evocative artwork for the interior and cover of this book. Amy McFrederick, OP for composing a piece of music, which captured the spirit of the circle process.

... Mary McCann, IHM for not only her wisdom as a Design Team member and author of the team's reflective story, but also her unswerving belief and support that what was arising in me regarding impasse and this project was from God.

... Mary Jo Klick—co-editor of this book and a collaborator with me for many years, who was one of the first who understood the vision and told me to go for it—for placing at the service of the project her many skills in administration, fund-raising, writing, editing, and hospitality, and for her willingness to work so closely with me on the day-to-day tasks.

My deep gratitude extends to my being able to call all of them friends.

I also want to thank the many religious congregations and foundations whose generosity has helped to finance the *Engaging Impasse* project. Without their willingness to risk funding this unusual project, the circle gatherings and CRUCIBLE FOR CHANGE never would have been realized.

I am especially indebted to my own religious congregation, the Sisters, Servants of the Immaculate

Heart of Mary, Monroe, Michigan, for their belief in me, the project, and this book—and for the support my sisters show in so many ways.

One individual whose initial and ongoing support for the *Engaging Impasse* project was very significant merits special acknowledgment. She was a donor, a participant, and a member of the Institute's newly formed board. Nancy O'Connor, CSJ from Orange, California, died unexpectedly on August 1, 2004. I will miss her vision, insight, and friendship. She is now with us in the greater circle of life.

Mary Jo and I are grateful to Jean Cmolik, CSJ, who lent her editorial skills to the initial reading of the book, and to Elise D. García for her skillful final editing.

We are especially grateful to Carol Coston, OP, Elise D. García, and the other members of the Board of Directors of Santuario Sisterfarm who created Sor Juana Press, for publishing CRUCIBLE FOR CHANGE.

I also want to thank Stephen Glodek, SM, Dan Daley, and Michael Culliton for their early consultation and advice.

Finally, I want to thank Sandra Schneiders, IHM, Beatrice Bruteau, and Constance FitzGerald, OCD for their willingness to share the wisdom of their contemplative insights during the planning and implementation of the circles.

Nancy Sylvester, IHM

ENGAGING IMPASSE PARTICIPANTS

The seventy-two participants in the *Engaging Impasse* project, including the Design Team, were: Renee Adamany, CSJ • Marcia Allen, CSJ • Jean Alvarez • Margaret Anderson, OP • Arlene Ashack, IBVM • Gilmary Bauer, RSM • Mary-beth Beres, OP • Susan Borgel, CPPS • Patricia Bruno, OP • Jane Burke, SSND • Janet Burkhart, HM • Helen Marie Burns, RSM • Simone Campbell, SSS • Judith Cauley, CSJ • Nancy Conway, CSJ • Marie Cooper, RJC • Patricia Daly, OP • Jennifer Discher • Rhea Emmer, CSA • Durstyne Farnan, OP • Mary Chris Fellerhoff, CSA • Maureen Fenlon, OP • Arlene Flaherty, OP • Margaret Galiardi, OP • Carmel García, CSJ • Patricia Gillis • Suzanne Golas, CSJP • Mary Ellen Gondeck, SSJ • Katherine Gray, CSJ • Mary Katherine Hamilton, IHM • Toni Harris, OP • Mary Hawk • Patty Hawk • Linda Haydock, SNJM • Valerie Heinonen, OSU • Mary Ann Hinsdale, IHM • Jenny Howard, SP • Mary Hunt • Rita Keegan, MM • Mary Jo Klick • Alexandra Kovats, CSJP • Pat Kozak, CSJ • Elizabeth Lavelle, CSJ • Mary McCann, IHM • Joellen McCarthy, BVM • Kathy McFaul • Reg McKillip, OP • Rose Mary Meyer, BVM • Mary Mollison, CSA • Judy Molosky, CSJ • Toni Nash, CSJ • Mary Jo Nelson, OLVM • Peggy Nolan, BVM • Nancy O'Connor, CSJ • Virginia Pfau, IHM • Constance Phelps, SCL • Catherine Pinkerton, CSJ • Ruthmary Powers, HM • Rosanne Rustemeyer, SSND • Susan Schorsten, HM • Gerry Sellman, SCMM • Elinor Shea, OSU • Carole Shinnick, SSND • Patricia Siemen, OP • Jean Stokan • Margaret Swedish • Nancy Sylvester, IHM • Carolyn Teter, CSJ • Mary Jean Traeger, OP • Teresa Tuite, OP • Mary Waskowiak, RSM • Mary Ann Zollmann, BVM.

ENGAGING IMPASSE SUPPORTERS

The supporters of the *Engaging Impasse* project include: Congregation of St. Agnes ACTS Fund, Fond du Lac, Wisconsin • Dominican Sisters, Houston, Texas • Franciscan Sisters of Allegany, St. Bonaventure, New York • Franciscan Sisters of Our Lady of Perpetual Help, St. Louis, Missouri, Ministry Grant Fund • Our Lady of Victory Missionary Sisters, Huntington, Indiana • Sisters of Charity, Cincinnati, Ohio • Sisters of Charity of Our Mother of Mercy, Detroit, Michigan, Solidarity Funds Committee • Sisters of Charity of the Blessed Virgin Mary, Dubuque, Iowa • Sisters of Charity of the Incarnate Word, Houston, Texas • Sisters of Loretto, Englewood, Colorado, The Loretto Community Special Needs Fund • Sisters of Mercy of the Americas • Sisters of Mercy of the Americas, Detroit, Michigan Region • Sisters of Providence, St.-Mary-of-the-Woods, Indiana • Sisters of St. Joseph, Cleveland, Ohio • Sisters of St. Joseph, Concordia, Kansas, St. Joseph Foundation • Sisters of St. Joseph, Kalamazoo, Michigan • Sisters of St. Joseph, Orange, California • Sisters of St. Joseph of Peace, Washington, D.C. • Sisters of St. Joseph of Peace Western Province, Bellevue, Washington • Sisters of the Holy Cross, Notre Dame, Indiana • Sisters of the Humility of Mary, Villa Maria, Pennsylvania • Sisters, Servants of the Immaculate Heart of Mary, Monroe, Michigan • Springfield (Illinois) Dominicans • The John and Sally Sommers Fund, Chicago, Illinois • The Louisville Institute, Louisville, Kentucky • The Wheaton Franciscans, Wheaton, Illinois.

These words of thanks would be incomplete without acknowledging the importance of a Native American story to the project. A frosted bowl I found in Portland, Oregon, with an image sketched in clear glass of a Native American  petroglyph, named *She Who Watches*, became a significant symbol for our circle gatherings.

In days past, according to the legend, the chief of a village was a woman who sat watching all that went on. Her people lived well, had plenty to eat, and inhabited strong houses. One day, Coyote, the Trickster, warned the chief that a time was coming when women would no longer be chiefs. To protect the people against this loss and to make sure that the chief could forever keep watch over her people, Coyote changed her into stone.

During the circle gatherings, *She Who Watches* watched over us, held our space open, received all that we would say and feel, and was a constant presence and reminder of the Divine within our midst.

Everything Before Us Brought Us to This Moment

Nancy Sylvester, IHM

There are times in history when significant shifts in consciousness occur, upending all we know. We are living in such a time. Our assumptions about how the world works, who we are as humans on this planet, how we live with each other in our diversity, and why we are here are called into question, no longer providing the meaning and direction they had in an earlier time.

These changes and shifts permeate our lives—and there are widely differing interpretations of the effects and meaning of these shifts. As in the nursery rhyme, Humpty Dumpty has fallen off the wall and shattered. Some experience the shattering as dangerous, a threat to the world they know and love, and seek to put Humpty Dumpty back together again; others see futility in the effort and, further, see hope for creating a new and more just, non-violent, and sustainable world now that Humpty Dumpty is gone.

Impasse is at the crossroads of these conflicting views—at the foot of the wall where the scattered pieces lie.

For many of us who have stood at the foot of that wall, facing seemingly intractable issues involving the

Roman Catholic Church and our society, this place of impasse evokes frustration, fear, desolation, depression. It's a place we want to walk away from, not engage.

This book is about engaging impasse and seeing that as a crucible for change; a process that holds the potential for something new to emerge.

It is about facing one's own fears surrounding impasse—entering the "dark night" of the mystical tradition. It is about practicing contemplation, which the English mystics described as taking "a long, loving look at the real."[1]

The book focuses on the experiences of ecclesial and societal impasse faced by a particular group of U.S. women, leaders within religious congregations and social justice activists rooted in the Roman Catholic tradition, who participated in a yearlong process of communal contemplation and dialogue to *engage* impasse. It is a process conceived out of my experiences and facing my own fears.

As an activist for more than thirty years, I feared admitting powerlessness in the work for social justice. As a member of the presidency of the Leadership Conference of Women Religious (LCWR), which took me to the Vatican on a yearly basis, I feared facing the reality of impasse in ecclesial conversations.

To admit being at a place of impasse, a place of powerlessness to effect change, felt like a betrayal of the social justice activists with whom I had worked over the years and the women religious I represented in LCWR. To then want to *engage*—rather than *solve*—the impasse through a process of contemplation hinted at a real sell-out! What would happen to passion? To action?

Even as I worried about this, I knew through my own spiritual journey and studies, that this is where I was—in the midst of impasse. It seemed to confront me everywhere, revealing the larger influences at work in all of us and in our world. These influences include the insights of quantum physics, the new cosmology, Earth spirituality, contextual theologies—*i.e.*, feminist theology, eco-theology, liberation theology—and the emerging reality of globalization.

To understand more comprehensively why Humpty Dumpty can't be put back together again and the powerful forces that shape our individual and collective experiences of impasse, I invite you to explore with me the historic, scientific, and social underpinnings at work in our shifting worldviews.[2]

OUR CURRENT WORLDVIEW: ROOTED IN PATRIARCHY AND NEWTONIAN ORDER

The planetary situation in which we find ourselves today is desperate. In the United States, fear and terror have defined our lives since September 11, 2001, blinding us to the underlying causes fueling violent attacks. Wars dominate the African continent and the Middle East. Worldwide, poverty increases as the concentration of wealth intensifies. Racism, sexism, and homophobia keep us divided. The growing commodification of humans and all other forms of life are radically diminishing the dignity of everyone and everything. And underlying all this is the ecological devastation that is rapidly threatening the very life of our planet, Earth.

How did we get to this state of affairs?

It is impossible to answer that question completely, but important insights emerge by examining the power of worldviews or paradigms. Like the air we breathe, we aren't always aware of the worldviews underlying the assumptions or values that give shape to our political, economic, cultural, and religious systems.

Major shifts in consciousness generate new worldviews. But these do not come often and when they do, they take years to filter down to our everyday life. Not all shifts break totally with the past. The most recent shift in consciousness, which took place about four hundred years ago, commonly called the Enlightenment, built upon the patriarchal mindset that has been with us for several millennia. Today both are undergoing a major shift. To understand the importance of the new shift in consciousness, we must examine the current prevailing worldview.

Patriarchy is a way of viewing the

> Our assumptions about how the world works, who we are as humans on this planet, how we live with each other in our diversity, and why we are here are called into question, no longer providing the meaning and direction they had in an earlier time.

world that biases the male experience. Patriarchy is a model of social organization that assures men have control and dominant power within social and religious structures. It is a model of social organization that has prevailed in many cultures throughout the world.

During the past millennium, as the Western world became dominant, the experience of the Euro-Christian male became normative, as did "his" way of viewing the world. For years, our history books reflected this bias as normative in describing the "great explorations" by Spaniards, Italians, and Portuguese and their "discovery" of land. This way of viewing the world gave support to the conquering of new lands and people—so-called "savages," who in fact were the heirs of complex societies developed over centuries, rich in religious and ethical traditions, agricultural practices, art, language, and even astronomy and architecture, among many.

The Church accompanied the explorers in order to convert the "heathens" or "pagans," essentially sanctioning their exploitative mission, which was to satisfy the insatiable quest for wealth of their powerful patrons. Since the Euro-Christian man felt he was sanctioned to dominate nature, it was a small stretch to feel justified in dominating and exploiting these "savages" and "heathens," simply by viewing them as less than human and therefore more like nature.

The time of the explorers was followed by a new era of scientific inquiry, beginning some 400 years ago, that reshaped the dominant Western worldview. This new worldview was rooted in the then-revolutionary physics of Isaac Newton and his colleagues, who based their thinking and inquiry on observation and reductionism. The scientific method they developed became the only true way of seeing reality; its hallmarks were simplicity, determinism, and predictability. It was a mechanistic way of thinking about the world where matter could be reduced to discrete pieces and observed in isolation from other matter and its environment. The whole could be understood by dissecting the parts. Change could be traced in a linear fashion to cause and effect. The observer and the observed were separate and detached; observation was the criterion for objectivity.[3]

The philosophy of René Descartes also contributed to this new worldview, or paradigm. Descartes and his followers emphasized the role of reason. Dualistic thinking, either/or ways of approaching reality prevailed, with one side of the dualism valued over the other: male over female; spirit over matter; human over nature; reason over emotions. Theology and religious experience were relegated to a purely private, subjective realm, as were other ways of knowing.

Belief in reason and science gave us an uncritical belief in progress. Progress was good no matter what its consequences. Those who asked critical or ethical questions about some aspects of this progress were dismissed. Progress for those who were in privileged places of power was the engine that drove prosperity.

The scientific revolution that began 400 years ago has led to a technological know-how rivaled by no other epoch in human history. The benefits and the costs of this revolution have been experienced, albeit disproportionately, across geographical and national boundaries. The Newtonian understanding of reality and how the universe works has shaped most of the cultural, economic, and political systems of our time. The Newtonian worldview has had implications for every aspect of life, although it has taken decades to be understood and embodied in all our institutions, systems, and ways of thinking.

Today, we witness both the fruits and the destructive consequences of the Newtonian worldview—and we see its basic tenets being challenged by a new worldview. This new paradigm is also being shaped by scientific inquiry, as well as by the insights and learnings of the major social movements of the past century. But this time, the emerging worldview is shattering even the millennia-old bedrock of patriarchy.

OUR EMERGING WORLDVIEW:
AS COHESIVE AND CHAOTIC AS THE UNIVERSE

At the turn of the twentieth century, Albert Einstein and other physicists ushered in the second scientific revolution through their work in quantum physics, which challenged the prevailing Newtonian assumptions of how the world works. Today, bits of matter are no longer seen in isolation from each other; instead, the universe is seen as a web of relationships subtly interconnected. Rather than simply dissecting to discern the whole, scientists now also observe the patterns that emerge when parts combine and cooperate to form a new whole that is revealed to be greater than the sum of its parts. The overall environment or context is critical to understanding, under this emerging new paradigm.

The "new science" tells us that change happens abruptly, dramatically, rapidly, often taking a leap beyond what came before. Human and nature are not in opposition but are interconnected and of the same stuff. The distinction between observer and observed is blurred and minimized; the scientist interacts and participates in the system under study. The hallmarks of the new physics are indeterminism, nonlinearity, and acausality; it speaks of fractals, wave/particles, quantum leaps, and chaos; it is a both/and way of thinking. The new paradigm shaped by these assumptions is beginning to permeate our lives, impelling us to ask new questions about the world in which we live.[4]

These new understandings about physics and the whole new worldview they have ushered in have been augmented by discoveries concerning the origin and unfolding of our universe and our role as humans in that unfolding—what many refer to as the "new cosmology."

In the early 1930s, Einstein observed a phenomenon that Edwin Hubble had been tracking through his telescope in nightly observations at Mount Wilson—the movement of galaxies away from each other at a rate in direct relation to the distance between them. Hubble's studies bore "the signature of cosmic expansion."[5] Some fifteen years earlier, Einstein's theory of general relativity had predicted something "strange and disturbing," implying that "the universe as a whole could not be static."[6] Since this was a "completely novel idea, and one for which there was, at the time, no observational evidence whatsoever," Einstein modified his equations with a "cosmological constant," restoring the universe to its static vastness.[7]

As Hubble's studies revealed, the universe in fact is dynamic, expanding in such a way that the distance between any two galaxies increases in time at a rate proportionate to the distance between them. It took most of the rest of the century for scientists finally to conclude, within the last thirty years or so, that the universe probably had a beginning as an unimaginably dense "singularity" of matter/energy. They postulate that the origins of the universe date back some 13.7 billion years, with an explosion of energy powerful enough to send the matter flying apart for billions of years into the future.[8] This theory of the origin of the universe is called the "big bang," or, more elegantly, the "flaring forth." The basic elements needed for life to emerge on this planet, some ten billion years later, were birthed in that first fiery explosion. Earth and our solar system evolved out of the remnants of a supernova, holding all the possibilities of life as we know it. Many scientists stand in awe and acknowledge that reason alone cannot comprehend this phenomenon. "Increasingly, scientists see evolution systemically and ecologically as the simultaneous and intertwined co-evolution of all Earth's species.... Each species helps shape every other, and each is shaped by the others."[9]

This new "Universe Story" is changing not only our operating cosmology but also how we as humans understand our relationship to Mother Earth. Understanding the human species in relationship to all species as a part of the web of life challenges the view of the human in dominant relation over nature that prevailed in the Newtonian worldview.

The discoveries of quantum physics and the new cosmology, together with insights born of the civil rights, feminist, environmental, and peace movements, as well as the growing grassroots challenge to globalization around the world, are providing the underpinnings of the emerging worldview. I believe it is in integrating these new perspectives in our lives that some of us are coming up against impasse in our work with individuals and institutions in Church and society.

WOMEN GATHER TO ENGAGE IMPASSE

In the context of this seismic shifting of world-views and from the ground of experience of the conflict and pain that arises from widely differing ways of acting and thinking in this in-between time, seventy-two women said, "yes," to an invitation to participate in a process of engaging the resulting impasse.

The women who participated in the circles shared a common religious tradition, Roman Catholicism, and were influenced by the call of the Second Vatican Council, which took place in the early 1960's, to discern the "signs of the times" and interpret them in light of the Gospel. We were inspired by later Church statements that "action on behalf of justice and participation in the transformation of the world fully appears to us as constitutive dimensions to the preaching of the Gospel."[10]

We have worked among the exploited and marginalized within Church and society, challenging the Church to embody the values of equality, participation, non-hierarchical modes of authority—values born of modernity, democratic societies, and our experience as women. We also have been involved in challenging political and economic institutions to embrace policies respecting the dignity of all life, equality for women, nonviolent responses to war, equitable distribution of resources, and the survival of the planet—values reflected in the Gospel and Catholic social teaching.

Feminism also has shaped us and our faith. We see the effects of patriarchy in the formulations of doctrine, in teachings on sexual morality, in the rules regarding who can be the official faith leader in Eucharistic celebrations, and in the language about God.

Study, as well, has had an impact. Many of us have been educating ourselves about the new cosmology, with some coming to embrace an Earth spirituality that sees the human in a new light—as belonging to Earth, as one of many species that evolved out of the same stardust. These insights are providing a deeper and richer context for our lives and for exploring our faith tradition.

Yet, it is in integrating these values and insights into our lives and into the structures and systems of our lives, that we have experienced impasse or powerlessness.

Patricia Bruno, OP continues to struggle as a preacher who is not allowed to preach in her Church. Joellen McCarthy, Peggy Nolan, and Mary Ann Zollmann, the BVM leadership team, were left unsettled by a compromise between their mutual desire to claim their own authority in hosting a workshop to address issues concerning homosexuality and to remain in relationship with their bishop, who objected to the presenters. Elinor Shea, OSU tried to create a new type of ministry, post Vatican II, that would serve as a link between the inner city and her congregation's college but abandoned it in the face of a restriction imposed for taking solemn vows—that she work "within our schools." Margaret Swedish, who spent years working to influence U.S. policy toward Central America, grieves at the seeming futility of so many martyred lives.

Mary Hunt, a feminist liberation theologian, sees all that she works for—equality for all, abundance of life on the planet, religions as sources of love and justice—violated by ecclesial and societal forces. Margaret Galiardi, OP and Rose Mary Meyer, BVM realize, after working for years to effect structural change, that a fatal flaw in our dominant institutions is a radical discontinuity with Earth. Pat Kozak, CSJ has experienced how power is held unevenly and exercised unfairly, and has come to sense that the institutions of which we are a part are terminally ill. Simone Campbell, SSS, a social justice lobbyist, lawyer, and poet, finds constant challenges of impasse in the legislative arena.

These stories reflect the experiences of all the participating women who, believing we were faithful to the Church's call after the Second Vatican Council and to our experiences as women, have felt the devastating impact of being ignored, devalued, and dismissed. The stories mirror the experiences of untold numbers of women and men who have been stopped short, coming face-to-face with impasse in the Church and in their work to create a more just society.

> Integrating the insights shaping the emerging worldview, with its new cosmology, raises new questions for those of us working for social justice and systemic change.

NOURISHING STARVED IMAGINATIONS

Integrating the insights shaping the emerging worldview, with its new cosmology, raises new questions for those of us working for social justice and systemic change. It invites us to act in ways that foster right relationships within this vast web of life; to work in ways that reflect unity within diversity; to understand that truth is shared and that dialogue will bring greater understanding; and to work for policies that reflect a commitment to the common good for the survival of the planet and all creation.

When I was honest with myself, I had to ask: Can the same tools of advocacy, protest, and organizing employed over decades do the job of transformation? Or is something else needed?

The words of Constance FitzGerald, OCD, a cloistered Carmelite in Baltimore, Maryland, spoke deeply to me.

> [O]ur time and place in history bring us face to face with profound societal impasse.... We can find no escape from the world we have built where the poor and oppressed cry out, where the earth and environment cry out, and where the specter of nuclear waste already haunts future generations.... Everything is just too complex, too beyond our reach. Yet it is only in the process of bringing the impasse to prayer, to the perspective of the God who loves us, that our society will be freed, healed, changed, brought to paradoxical new visions, and freed for nonviolent, selfless, liberating action, freed, therefore, for community on this planet earth.[11]

What seared my heart were the words, "...it is only in the process of bringing the impasse to prayer, to the perspective of the God who loves us that we will be freed for nonviolent, selfless, liberating action... freed for community on this planet earth."

> We need to tap into another way of knowing...

I realized our imaginations are starved. We cannot imagine new ways or simply think or strategize our way out of the old conceptual framework or worldview. We need to tap into another way of knowing, the kind of knowing that arises from our spirituality—a way of knowing that has been diminished by the prevailing worldview. We need to touch into the liberating spiritual impulse that is foundational to all the great religions.[12]

It was into this context that the project, *Engaging Impasse: Circles of Contemplation and Dialogue*, was born.

TURNING TO ANCIENT PRACTICES
TO ENGAGE THESE TIMES

The invitation to engage impasse was a call to enter into a process of communal contemplation and dialogue. Implicit in the invitation to *engage* impasse was the awareness that either/or ways of approaching social change created divisions, not right relationships. For the participating women, engaging impasse from a faith perspective acknowledged that, in the ecclesial arena, the very people with whom they experienced impasse often were individuals they respected and with whom they worked. Engaging impasse from a faith perspective also recognized that, in the work of social justice, one more weekend meeting to shape a grand strategy would not bring about the sought-after reforms.

Entering into communal contemplation and dialogue meant tapping into the rich contemplative/mystical traditions. In Catholicism, it is a tradition that begins with the desert fathers and mothers; continuing with Julian of Norwich and Meister Eckhart, who flourished in the Middle Ages; with the writings of Teresa of Avila, Catherine of Siena, and John of the Cross; and stretching into our own era with mystics like Therese of Lisieux and Thomas Merton.

Contemplation is a different form of prayer from the memorized prayers and visual meditations that many of us learned growing up. Contemplation is primarily awareness, a state of alertness to the present and to the stirrings of God within us, and in our world.

Contemplation invites us to conversion and to enter the very deep place within ourselves where we encounter our God. It is an intuitive and intimate experience of God in the everydayness of life. It is knowledge of God that comes from one's own experience, and it complements coming to know God through liturgical rituals, tradition, doctrine, books, and instruction.

> ...the kind of knowing that arises from our spirituality—
> a way of knowing that has been diminished by the prevailing worldview.

FitzGerald writes about the experience of impasse and how it can be understood within the contemplative tradition of St. John of the Cross and what he describes as the "dark night of the soul." This place of impasse opens us to the possibility of encountering God anew. It offers the possibility of more radical responses; of transformation and conversion; and of renewing our passion for the Gospel vision of justice and peace.

I believe that the crossroads of history and time at which we now find ourselves, facing extraordinary challenges, calls us to this form of prayer. A danger, as one begins a contemplative prayer life, is to think that it is a concentration on self, the well being of one's soul, and the privatization of religion. Nothing is further from reality. From the depths of contemplation comes renewed action. Contemplation can free us from many constraints, including our own selfishness and ego-driven ways. Contemplation moves us to action, to resistance, to imagining new ways of being and acting.

Engaging impasse through a process of contemplation and dialogue resonated with each of the women who accepted the invitation. It called on a desire to open oneself to the stirrings of God, and to do so together.

As you read the stories, you will see that impasse was understood in a variety of ways, and from very personal to cosmic dimensions. The process we used to engage impasse accommodated these differences, allowing for individual and communal transformation. Mary McCann, IHM skillfully captures the collective reflections of the Design Team about the process, the planning, and the learnings.

Although it is hard to capture precisely in words, something significant happened to the participants and planners. We began to see that we were able to release the oppressive power that situations of impasse or the people involved had over us—and we were able to glimpse new ways of being and acting.

This book is a sharing of the experiences of engaging impasse of a particular group of women. While the details of their experiences may be unique, I believe the larger contours of their stories will resonate with many people, perhaps including you. I invite you to read the book with this in mind, using the reflection questions at the end of the book to deepen your own engagement with the stories. You may want to read the stories sequentially or choose a perspective that attracts you. Each of the stories tells the experience of the circles from the perspective of the author and how it affected her life, work, or ministry. I encourage you to see where you are drawn and to linger there; to see what speaks to your heart.

My hope is that the book conveys the power of the communal contemplative experience in engaging impasse in your life and that it invites you to become more aware of the competing worldviews within yourself and in those around you. I hope the shared stories invite you to see engaging impasse as a crucible for change. I pray, in the end, that we will be freed through this ancient process of surrender "for nonviolent, selfless, liberating action, freed, therefore, for community on this planet earth."[13]

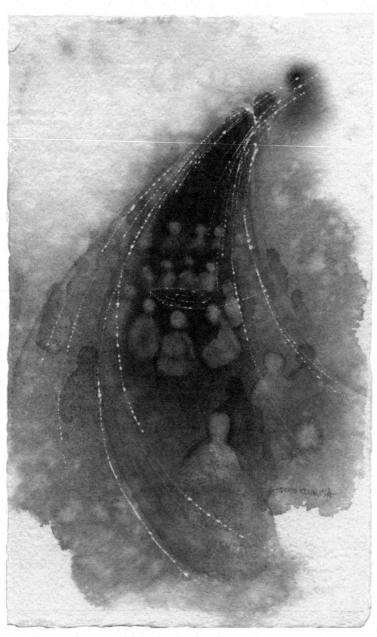

Communal Contemplation

Being Present to a Process

Mary McCann, IHM

Between January 2003 and February 2004, seventy-two U.S. women participated in a ten-to-twelve month process entitled *Engaging Impasse: Circles of Contemplation and Dialogue*. Initiated by Nancy Sylvester, IHM and assisted by a Design Team, the process invited participants to bring experiences of impasse in Church and society into an arena of shared contemplation and dialogue. Primarily middle-aged and Euro-American, the women, nine lay and sixty-three religious, were rooted in the Catholic faith tradition, progressive in orientation, and advocates for justice in Church and society. Invitees, most of whom were known by one or more members of the Design Team, were introduced to the vision, experiences, and hopes of the *Engaging Impasse* process through letters, accompanying materials, the project web site, and personal contact.

This is the story of the evolution and fruits of this experience—in the initiator of the project; in the project designers; and in the participants as interpreted by the Design Team. It is the story of women choosing to trust in the Divine who beckons us toward an unknown future. It is the story of naming, entering, and embracing impasse experiences in an environ-

19

ment and through a process in which listening to the Divine within oneself, others, and in experience is the primary call and the founda-

> Listening to the Divine within oneself, others, and in experience is the primary call and the foundation of dialogue.

tion of dialogue. The story begins with one woman experiencing the limits of human efforts and gradually allowing the Divine to beckon her to new and deeper spiritual waters.

The Call

The *Engaging Impasse* project arose out of Nancy Sylvester's own experience of impasse in Church and society, arising from fifteen years of passionate commitment to social justice expressed in her work at NETWORK, a national Catholic social justice lobby, from 1977 to 1992, and three years in the presidency of the Leadership Conference of Women Religious (LCWR), from 1998 to 2001. In both arenas, societal and Church, Nancy experienced impasse—a sense of futility, of powerlessness to effect change, of sensing no way out of the prevailing systems which she perceived as unjust. Additionally, she felt that none of the traditional ways of effecting transformation were working; that no one had an adequate answer or strategy.

Gradually Nancy recognized that the call was to go deeper; to trust the Divine within who beckons us from a future we cannot yet envision to imagine new ways of being and acting in the world. Thus in a memo to the Design Team in January 2002, Nancy said, "the experience of impasse invites me to face my power-lessness and as a person of faith to trust in the power of God ... for me impasse is not hopeless or negative. There is hope in entering the impasse."

As Nancy prepared her presidential address to the National Assembly of LCWR in August 2000, these realizations were present to her. With the support of trusted others, she found the courage to give voice to what was welling up within her. Delivering her address to the nearly one thousand LCWR members gathered in Albuquerque, New Mexico, she shared her insight that U.S. women religious are in an impasse with Church officials in Rome. What LCWR leaders and members experience as gifts to the Church and world continue to be sources of deep conflict with some Vatican officials.

In her address, Nancy reflected on how women religious have taken seriously the Church's call to renewal and have given expression to a form of religious life situated in and both critical and expressive of the culture and values of the United States. She recounted the empowering impact upon LCWR members when in 1971 the international synod of bishops proclaimed that "action on behalf of justice and participation in the transformation of the world fully appear to us as constitutive dimensions to the preaching of the Gospel."[14] She described how women religious in the ensuing decades have become women speaking and acting on behalf of justice; women seeking the transformation of the Church and world; women claiming their full humanity, expecting to be heard, expecting to be participants in decision-making in the Church, particularly when it affects their own lives, institutions, and ministries. But as Nancy observed, it is precisely in these areas that deep conflict persists. She voiced her conviction that the impasse experience was calling LCWR leaders and members to a place of deep prayer and contemplation.[15]

The assembly expressed resonance with these insights by giving her a heartfelt standing ovation. Nancy's naming of LCWR's long and painful truth breathed courage and hope into the assembly. Her invitation to contemplation spoke to members' deepest source of energy and vision and resulted in a two-year commitment to shared contemplation by the LCWR membership.

Testing an Intuition

The reception by LCWR members to Nancy's address confirmed that she was naming and addressing a deep need. She brought her experience to prayer and consulted with contemplatives, experts in the field of dialogue, and others. They helped her hone the vision/dream of forming "circles of contemplation and dialogue" for those who were experiencing impasse in societal and ecclesial arenas.

Feeling the need to test further her intuition with women sensitive to impasse issues and gifted in facilitation, spiritual growth and direction, left-brain and artistic processes, and research, Nancy invited eight women to reflect with her on the direction she was considering. In January 2002, we met in Cleveland, Ohio, over four days and experienced a synergy of vision and creativity that effectively marked the launching of the *Engaging Impasse* project.

Nancy began by sharing the evolution of her vision, including her growing clarity that the circles would be composed of leaders of religious communities and justice activists rooted in the Catholic faith tradition. Her transparent desire to be faithful to the Spirit, combined with the timeliness and spiritual rootedness of the proposal, unleashed similar openness in the eight of us gathered with her. What followed was a high energy, contemplatively rooted, playful and highly productive meeting. It was an experience of nine people, some meeting for the first time, tending a sacred trust. Through the intersection of our individual creative energies, we gave further shape and direction to the *Engaging Impasse* project.

We summarized the intent and processes of the project succinctly with this statement: "The project is designed as an environment and a process which invites the participants to enter sacred space to engage in unfolding the impasse by naming, entering, and embracing it through communal contemplation and dialogue." We imagined it as a ten-to-twelve month process in which participants would be energized and focused through three face-to-face, three-day gatherings. We imagined participants focused either on experiences of societal or ecclesial impasse. Between gatherings, we envisioned participants engaging in personal contemplative practice, as well as communal reflection facilitated by the project website and conversation board.

Importantly, the Design Team saw that the total environment needed to be supportive of communal contemplation and dialogue. We wanted the schedule and space arrangements, as well as the process and rituals, to invite and knead the inner silence, relaxation, spaciousness, deep listening, self-awareness, and sense of community that would enable circle members to take the "long, loving look at the real" which is central to contemplative knowing. Thus we included experiences such as journaling, yoga, breathing practices, art, walking meditation, labyrinth, music, and parties for the participants.

Six of the nine women attending this meeting continued on the permanent Design Team: Marcia Allen, CSJ; Jean Alvarez; Nancy Conway, CSJ; Mary Jo Klick; Mary McCann, IHM; and Nancy Sylvester, IHM. The others eagerly offered their expertise in other ways. Dorothy Ettling, CCVI, worked on the research portion of the project. Doris Klein, CSA, artist, created the *Engaging Impasse* logo. Bette Moslander, CSJ, served as a backup facilitator and consultant.

DESIGNING *AND* ENGAGING IN THE PROCESS

The Design Team met for "planning intensives" prior to the beginning of each of the three gatherings. Meeting in a spirit of friendship and collaborative endeavor, rituals were woven into the fabric of each day. We then wrestled with translating the overall plans generated in the earlier exploratory meeting into the particulars we would be using in each of the gatherings. Creative, contemplative, committed energy was again in rich supply as we sought approaches conducive to the hoped-for outcomes: a release of deep spiritual energy; an experience of community; fresh imagination; new vision for continuing the work in ecclesial and societal arenas.

We soon discovered the value of doing ourselves what we would ask participants to do. For instance, in planning for the first circle gatherings, Design Team members wrote and read aloud our own stories of impasse, experiencing the challenge, the vulnerability, and the power of doing this in a group that was actively and deeply listening. In each planning session, we reflected on what happened in the prior gathering. As we created the next approach, we practiced it among ourselves. This helped us see how what we were proposing fit our goals. It also invited some profound personal insights and a deepening appreciation of one another's struggles with impasse experiences. It helped us hone our use and explanation of the process with circle members. We recognized that we worked in a spirit of contemplation and engaged in dialogue throughout our discussions. We did not, however, actively experiment with the formal dialogue techniques we introduced to participants as we had done with other processes. These techniques involved slowing down the pace, trying to make conscious each other's assumptions, building on each other's insights rather than speaking what one might have previously prepared, dealing with difference, and formulating the communal question for dialogue. In retrospect, we wondered whether doing so might have enhanced our use of dialogue during the circle gatherings.

REFLECTIONS ON THE CIRCLE GATHERINGS

The participants were organized into six circles, three focusing on societal impasse and three on ecclesial impasse. Each gathering of the six circles was designed to enfold the prior one and also broaden and deepen our engagement with the experience of impasse. Thus, in the first gathering we accessed personal stories of impasse; in the second we deepened our understanding of the causes of impasse; in the final gathering we brought to contemplation and dialogue the insights we had gleaned during the prior months.

Four members of the Design Team met consistently with each of the six circles. They both enabled the movement of the process and participated in it. This dual functioning was a deliberate choice of the Design Team, arising from our desire to experience the process and not simply observe and lead it.

FIRST CIRCLE GATHERING:
ACCESSING THE STORIES OF IMPASSE

The first circle gathering focused on accessing more deeply participants' personal stories of impasse within either the ecclesial or societal arenas. We engaged those experiences communally in a contemplative atmosphere and reflected on the experiences in the broader context of our faith. The process invited participants to sit at the feet of their own impasse story and of one another's stories—hearing and feeling deeply the painful struggle; the floundering; the setbacks; the futility alongside the noble visions and longings and hard years of work. It asked them to hear in themselves and others the various

> The process invited participants to sit at the feet of their own impasse story and of one another's stories—

responses: the anger; the fear; the self-blame and recrimination; the desperate activity; the discouragement; the apathy; and the projections of blame and hostility on various others.

The process invited the simple direct telling of each person's impasse story—seeking contemplative understanding not interpretation. That is, circle members were asked to take a long receptive look at their impasse experience—its details, the feelings it evoked, the effect it had on them—and then to communicate that simply and directly to other circle members. It asked risk-taking and vulnerability of everyone—both of which Nancy had exemplified in her opening remarks for each new circle—and built trust within the circle. For the Design Team it revealed the way forward: follow the pain and the wisdom of the

—individual stories became universal stories....

impasse stories; bring them into the light of communal contemplation; and over the three circle gatherings, name, engage, and embrace the impasse.

In our later reflections, one member of the team, an experienced spiritual director, offered insights, which resonated in the rest of us. She said that what she heard in participants' stories can best be described as desolation—a chaotic hodge-podge of feeling and action/inaction which leaves the person alienated and disconnected from her own sense of purpose and identity. The question, she said, seemed to be not necessarily how to change the darkness to light or the impasse to non-impasse but rather how to change a desolate journey in the darkness into one of consolation, even in the darkness and impasse. As community grew among us, as contemplation and dialogue deepened, as the circles continued to meet, individual stories became universal stories of human engagement with finitude; a dynamic of restorative hope began to emerge and unfold.

The Design Team also agreed that extended communal silences—simply being in each other's company in the silences—released some powerful energy and awareness in the participants. It allowed them to touch into some very destructive experiences without the need to resolve or justify them. One of us spoke of observing some very self-assured, very competent women give themselves over to the messiness and mystery of these experiences. They understood that in allowing themselves to touch into the pain of their impasse story in a new way, they need not do anything other than believe that somehow God is revealing God's self.

Second Circle Gathering:
Understanding the Causes of Impasse

The second circle gathering was designed to deepen our understanding of the causes of impasse. As individuals we accessed how we are stuck in the impasse; what holds us there and how we are complicit in our experiences of impasse. We engaged in dialogue around these experiences of being bound, bringing our deepening communal understanding to contemplation.

The Design Team deliberately chose to place the focus on the impasse experience of circle members. Assuming we already knew how to analyze, fixate, and plan our lives in response to the aggrieving party's actions/behavior, we believed that the emotions evoked in us by impasse would be the best starting place for acknowledging complicity. Building on work from earlier in the process and sensing that frustrated desire/intentionality is at the heart of impasse, we asked participants to identify the emotion most evoked in them

> We accessed how we are stuck in the impasse; what holds us there and how we are complicit in our experiences of impasse.

by the experience of impasse. In a process that invited deepening explorations, each woman asked herself several times why impasse evoked that emotion in her. For many, this approach revealed a complexity of motivations and issues which were suggestive of their complicity in the impasse. As the design developed, this starting place enabled participants to touch into significant, sometimes dark and disturbing, awareness of what was stirring in them as they encountered impasse in Church or society.

We took that awareness into silent contemplative sitting; into a communal walking meditation; into individual use of the labyrinth; into yoga, journaling, and dialogue. Interestingly, the two movements into dialogue, which we considered central to the second gathering, were challenging and often hard to assess in terms of their fruitfulness. It remains unclear to us whether this is related to our facilitation of the dialogue process, the learning curve in the circles regarding formal dialogue, or the focus on complicity in the impasse.

Significantly, however, the final ritual designed by the circle participants evidenced that the women had in fact contemplated, acknowledged, and engaged their complicity in impasse. The rituals—through prayer, symbol, body, and song—voiced grief and mourning; asked for forgiveness; expressed hope for liberation and transformation. These rituals were powerful expressions of, turning to the Divine in the darkness of oneself and of impasse. We wonder whether a kinesthetic, visual intelligence rather than a verbal, linguistic intelligence assisted the deepening we experienced through the second circle experience. By the time of the third gatherings some months later it seemed clear, through comments and references to what had gone on in their lives, that everyone had further integrated a sense of her own complicity in the impasse.

Third Circle Gathering: Contemplating Our Stance in Impasse

The overall goal of the third circle gathering was to bring to contemplation how we choose to be with and/or in the impasse. We engaged in dialogue regarding these insights, learnings, and wisdom in hopes of moving forward. We deepened our personal and communal strategies, disciplines, practices, and prophetic actions as to how to engage impasse.

The challenge in designing the third and final gathering was to stay mindful that our purpose was not to resolve impasse but to engage and embrace it. Introductory comments by Nancy addressed this assumption and, with some humor at times, participants accepted our assumption. In line with our goals, we planned this session so as to support the further release of deep spiritual energy and the building of community, while eliciting fresh imagination and new vision for the work.

Significant time was devoted to enabling individuals to articulate and clarify what was shifting in them regarding engaging impasse. Some of the shifts repeated many times were: the importance of naming the struggle; a radical shift in consciousness; a surrender to who I really am;

> Our purpose was not to resolve impasse but to engage and embrace it.

a profound letting go; a yielding to the divine energy; accepting powerlessness; radical openness of a loving, anguishing heart; giving up the attachment to winning the struggle; surrendering my own Grand Plan; breathing deeply; seeing the other as human. These and other shifts then became the foundation for deepening our communal contemplation and dialogue.

We then invited participants into deep contemplation focused on the question: What am I being invited to surrender in prayer to the God who loves me so as to liberate/free me to be and act in new ways? This was enabled by a long evocative ritual, which began in a communal setting and then invited individuals to an extended time of contemplation. The ritual used poetry and a long meditative chant by Jennifer Berezan to draw us into a solemn interior space. The chant's hauntingly beautiful words, "She Who Hears the Cries of the World," spoke to the desires and frustrations of women immersed in their impasse experiences.

After the group ritual, circle members were invited to maintain a spirit of vigil until the next morning using whatever means enabled them to contemplate the question posed earlier. As one means of assisting the vigil experience, our circle space was transformed into several different prayer centers, including spaces centered in Christian, Eastern, and cosmological themes. In our follow-up sharing the next morning, a quiet centeredness marked each person's sharing of her learnings, insights, and wisdom. The yoga session that followed acted as a bridge furthering the surrender process and opening participants' energy to new ways of being and imagining. We felt it was our best experience of yoga, serving a particular moment in the process, and it opened our eyes as to how to better integrate yoga into the first two circle gatherings.

Assisted by a guided meditation, we then imagined what a new engaging impasse community might look like. What would it be centered in? What characteristics, practices, supports, symbols, and new activities would be signs of this new community? How would we know we were backsliding into old patterns of behavior?

In the conversations among participants, paradoxical patterns emerged. For example, participants desired to be deeply, fully engaged in the transformation of Church and society while also desiring and needing to be less busy, more contemplative, more centered in the Divine, more still, more vulnerable, more playful, more caring of themselves, more connected with friends and Earth. They wanted to care deeply about the outcomes of their efforts while also desiring to surrender their plans and strategies and the results of their efforts to the Divine. They intended to exercise power with humility; to express the unvarnished truth with an open and loving heart; to see themselves and their efforts within the creative, evolutionary activity of the universe. While recognizing how easy it is to slip into old patterns, they named and wanted to avoid the signs of backsliding: cynicism, demonizing the other, drivenness, boredom, overextension, paralysis. Some articulated a concern that in behaving in new ways they might lose their passion or their edge in doing the work of justice.

True to our conviction that communal contemplation involves the whole process, the final dinners of this third gathering became special feasts. They provided a forum to continue the energy and insights that had emerged in the course of the gatherings. After appropriate closure activities the following morning, each circle concluded with a simple, powerful, and integrative ritual.

In this final gathering, the Design Team experienced participants more rooted in their deepest selves and reclaiming their spiritual centers. This was evident in their recognizing and wanting to release ego-based behaviors; in accepting their complicity in their impasse experiences; and in their clear desires and efforts to yield to the Divine while they continued their various works. It was evident as they expressed what was shifting in them individually and as a community. It was expressed in the fruit of their extended individual prayer time and in how they imagined a new engaging impasse community functioning. It was also clear that their shared experience had forged deep bonds of community among them.

We realized through the final dinner conversations and through discussions on the final mornings that moving out beyond the circle experience presented a new set of challenges. The women wanted to continue acting according to their deepest desires in the midst of everyday pressures. Many spoke of wanting to stay in contact with one another to sustain the vision and behaviors they had come to value. This led the Design Team in our post-circles planning to encourage continuing dialogue using the electronic conversation board. We also planned issue-oriented follow-up gatherings. Participants, too, initiated contact and gatherings among themselves.

CLOSING OBSERVATIONS

We believe the *Engaging Impasse* process worked well in the pursuit of our goals. In hindsight it is hard to say which piece(s) of the process were most integral for participant growth because they were tightly interwoven one with the other, contributing to a flow of contemplative energy and awareness. Although individuals responded differently, according to their needs and attunements, there was a quite palpable release of spiritual energy and growth in community within each circle, along with important signs of fresh imagination and new vision emerging within the groups.

We celebrate our wisdom in saying that "communal contemplation" is the whole process, extending through the three gatherings. Everything contributed to our taking "a long, loving look at the real." Thus every aspect of experience, personal and communal, within the circle gatherings and back home, was reverenced as sacred and revelatory; no dichotomies were introduced. Participants caught the spirit of this and honored it wholeheartedly. It seemed to meet a hunger, as well as to serve the vision of the Design Team. We believe it allowed us to gradually experience Amy McFrederick's stirring mantra sung over and over in our gatherings: God's silence had indeed "seeped into the darkness" of our impasse experiences, "birthing the new, opening a way to peace." [16]

We celebrate the courage, integrity, and deep longings of the women with whom we journeyed in the six circles. Their willingness to name, engage, and embrace impasse in circles of communal contemplation and dialogue was and remains a striking manifestation of their intense commitment—and a source of very rich learning and spiritual growth for us and them. Their continuing openness and surrender to the Divine as they work for the transformation of Church and society is a tremendous source of energy for us and for the planetary community.

In addition to being a member of the *Engaging Impasse* Design Team, Mary McCann IHM is a process consultant and writer with a particular interest in promoting sustainable living and community. Formerly the President of the IHM Sisters, Monroe, Michigan, (1994-2000) and a long-time educator and spiritual director, Mary also enjoys photography, the outdoors, and writing poetry.

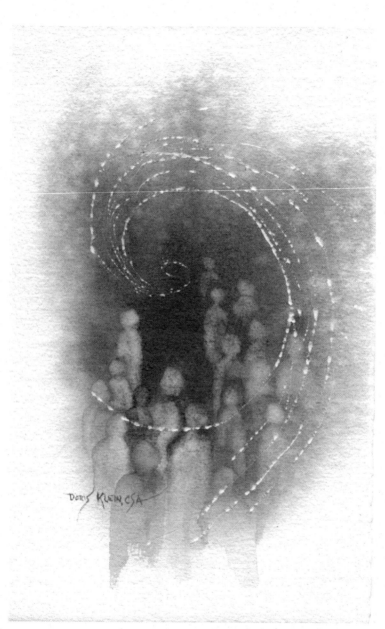

Deep Searching for Truth

One Inch Long, Many Miles Deep

Patricia Bruno, OP

About a year ago I read THE FORGOTTEN DESERT MOTHERS by Laura Swan. It's a small book, packed with stories about Desert Mothers, or *ammas*—women who lived their hermit lives in the desert or in "cells," small rooms attached to a house or church in the center of the city. Each of the *ammas* Laura Swan chose for her study had her own distinct personality and gifts, and the wisdom each shared with her spiritual directees was included in the book. An insight of *Amma* Syncletica's was one of my favorites. She said the path to God is very difficult because it is only "one inch long, but a mile deep. The spiritual journey requires perseverance, steadfastness, remaining with commitments, and working through difficulties."[17]

Amma Syncletica's image of the path to God captured my imagination and stayed with me throughout the circle gatherings, as we "circle women" explored our lives and experiences of impasses, gently digging, as if excavating a holy site, and digging deep. Together, we metaphorically put on large sun hats and durable garden gloves. In one hand we held our familiar family trowels. In the other, we grasped large soft brushes that would help us gently dust away the layers of accumulated soil that covered our stories.

The invitation to be part of an *Engaging Impasse* circle came at a good time for me, as some major shifts were taking place in my life. It felt like an invitation inspired by the Spirit to whom I had been praying for direction. Although I didn't know where this exploration was going to take me, my "Yes" was wholehearted. In fact, I chuckled one day when I heard myself refer to the process as *embracing* impasse instead of engaging impasse. My misnomer revealed an unspoken, intuitive understanding of what this experience would eventually mean for me. Engaging impasse meant I had to first acknowledge it, listen to it, and indeed unearth some of my dormant understandings and intentionally buried feelings.

Before I began the process, I looked up the word "impasse" in the dictionary. I thought I knew what it meant, but I wanted to be sure. There it was: "a cul-de-sac, a predicament affording no obvious escape. Deadlock." Implied in the definition are a serious situation and an immense block. It's not just a casual detour, but a disagreement of substance, a roadblock that is seemingly immovable. Situations like these are complex and feelings run deep. There is often an inequality between or among the members involved, with one member being privileged to have the final word over another or others.

Addressing situations like these takes a great deal of energy and truthfulness—and that's what the circle gatherings challenged us to do. We had layers of information, strata of relationships and motives to consider and explore. Even though there were some common patterns in our stories of struggle, disappointment, and disillusionment, each had its own unique twist. Each story of conflict or injustice ran its course through our multi-layered social, political, and religious systems, requiring attentive listening as well as deep sharing.

Deep-digging is a tedious process. The soil can be hard, rocky, and resistant. The temptation is to reach for a large shovel instead of "troweling" the ground with care. The temptation is to search for the big treasures, the outstanding finds that everyone can admire and celebrate. But from the beginning—the letter of invitation, the initial preparatory readings, the very title: *Engaging Impasse*—we were reminded that this was not going to be an easy or superficial process. The rhythm of private prayer, community contemplation, circle dialogues, silence, and community-building celebrations were carefully designed. If we were going to dig deep and extract important understandings from the sharing of our stories, the process had to be done with care and reverence, for what we were exploring was holy ground.

> If we were going to dig deep and extract important understandings from the sharing of our stories, the process had to be done with care and reverence, for what we were exploring was holy ground.

It was within our small circle conversations that our stories of impasse were first told, listening with reverent curiosity and attentiveness. As we shared our own stories, we were encouraged to observe the images and feelings they evoked in us. As we listened, communities of trust began to take shape. Without this first step—a trusting and trustworthy community of listeners—our search for a deeper understanding of our experiences of impasses would have been thwarted. As we listened, common words began to emerge: disillusionment, anger, impatience, frustration, fear. We could hear in our new questions and insights the tentative trust developing. Our conversations also were inspirited by the buoyancy of good humor and the energy of supportive wise friends.

My Experience of Ecclesial Impasse Began Early and Continues

My own story—of struggling with impasse in the Church—started as a teenager. My parents, according to Church teaching, were lost souls. They were remarried and for them, there was no way out. I remember voicing an opposing point of view in religion class one day. The silence that followed was isolating. I also remember the profound conviction that in spite of what others taught, I was somehow correct in my understanding of the large scheme of things. This intuitive sense of God's unconditional love has under girded my spiritual life and justice ministry.

For over forty years I have worked in a variety of justice ministries. In the sixties, I worked with the United Farm Workers. Later, as the Promoter of Justice for our congregation, my passion was joined with those who worked for public sanctuary for Salvadoran and Guatemalan refugees. Then, in the nineties, wanting to explore some of the root causes of economic injustice, I began working with community loan funds and developed an economic-justice education program that examined common banking and lending practices. Recognizing the violence in each of these situations, I began studying and learning more about nonviolence. In response to our congregation's stance supporting nonviolence, I worked for four years with Pace e Bene, a Franciscan-based nonviolence movement. During this time, I studied the causes of violence, gave workshops on creative strategies for nonviolence, and collaborated on a book on nonviolence.

While engaged in these ministries, I was always conscious of the unjust structures within our Church—especially those impacting women's full recognition and participation in the ministries of the Church. Over the years, these unjust structures and Church teachings about the role of women have had a particular effect on me as a Dominican woman, creating a painful experience of impasse.

As a vowed member of a religious order known as the "Order of Preachers," the Church has formally accepted my vocation as a preacher. And as a Dominican, I love reading, studying, and praying with the Scriptures. I love teaching, preaching, and creating prayer rituals that help people become more grounded in God's mercy and forgiveness. Over the years, my studies and experiences have helped me grow in the ability to analyze the social and political contexts of our lives in light of Scripture and the social teachings of our Church. Our congregation's mission "to proclaim God's Word in our world…bringing the Gospel to bear with depth and compassion on the critical issues of our times..." also has helped form and inform my consciousness. Preaching out of the Scriptures, I have been encouraged by the vibrant spirituality of the Order and my own experiences to be a preacher of grace. Often this grace is most poignantly experienced in times of struggle, doubt, and insecurity— in times of tension and transition—in times of impasse.

The O.P. after my name is a reminder of the Dominican charism and responsibility to preach the Word when "convenient and inconvenient." The phrase refers not just to the obligation to preach when we may or may not feel like it; it embraces a more subtle meaning when applied to a Church where women's gifts are not fully recognized or appreciated. For women, it is *inconvenient* to preach in a Church that limits the times and places we can preach; that does not offer women full participation in her ministries; that suffers poor or unprepared homilies rather than permitting a layperson to proclaim a well-prepared word of faith and hope. This prejudice tugs at my self-worth, my self-confidence, and my vocation.

The struggle for me doesn't get easier as it continues; it remains as poignant today as the day it began. I still wonder: Who will proclaim God's word? If the Church excludes some who are qualified and gifted by the Spirit to preach, how will people come to know and experience God? In the Bible, God is described as a God of tenderness and compassion, slow to anger, rich in mercy and faithfulness; God's kindness lasts for a thousand generations. (Exodus 34:6) But who will know this God if there are not many of us proclaiming God's Word? It is here, in the midst of the "convenient and inconvenient" that the persistent, yet gentle, dusting of the soil reveals within its layers ancient truths about who is called to preach.

The details of my story might be different from yours, but in another way, many of our stories are very similar. Haven't we all struggled against injustice? Haven't we all wept with those who are overlooked, demonized, or marginalized? Haven't we all been scandalized by the unjust actions and policies of the Church? And, on the other hand, haven't we all wrestled with our own inner demons of self-doubt, unworthiness, impatience, aggression. Our inner voices seldom leave enough space for human error or miscalculation, for others or for ourselves.

THE POWER OF THE CIRCLES

So what happened in the circles? What difference have these yearlong gatherings and sharings made in my life? Can my experience be measured or weighed, charted or used for a PowerPoint presentation? If it were that easy, one of the wise women organizers would have written a book or called us together to share the "Secrets of Living Wisdom Well." But we all know it is not that easy. We know, too, as with all profound seeking, that the integrity of the process is an important part of the search for truth.

Each of the three sessions was carefully designed by our facilitators. Their nuanced and effective "conversation suggestions" soon became an integral part of our small and large circle sharing. New insights and learnings were acknowledged and integrated into the process. The findings from our slow-paced, small-circle conversations, where we gathered in groups of three to tell our stories, were shared with the larger circle of eleven women. Both in the large and small circle gatherings, we were encouraged to ask questions rather than make definitive statements. We learned to listen for our collective and individual assumptions and presumptions. We learned also to search trustingly for areas of incongruity or lack of clarity. Instead of trying to solve the "problem," we explored how our past experiences gave us the tools and expertise to work new territories of impasse.

The unearthing of our layered stories was like the field process that discovers ancient artifacts. A sensitive exploration reveals only the tip of "the find" at first, but when the soil is dusted carefully, even broken articles offer clues that will help explain our present situations in the light of past experiences. It takes time and patience, but when the ground of experience is worked with respect and acceptance, even resistant soil relinquishes surprising truths. Our times together refreshed previous learnings, yielded new insights, and raised inviting questions that still linger in my memory. These treasures I will continue to ponder.

I have come to understand the power of connecting and learning from our wisdom experiences. Our inner struggles can teach us how to address other experiences of impasse. The more we are able to confront our own inner fears, insecurities, and denials, the more strength and insight we will have to work with the incongruities that surround us. One of the women told a story of impasse that began more than thirty years ago. Its relevance, however, has not been diminished by time. In fact, time has helped her see the deeper connections. What began as social drinking later became an addiction to alcohol. Even though her friends encouraged her to seek help, it took some time for her to realize that she had no control over this internal impasse. The eventual realization of her powerlessness, the support of her friends, and a deep trust in God gave her the courage to begin and stay with the Twelve-Step Program. She knew the only way she could become free from this powerful addiction was to enter into the struggle. The only way out of this impasse was to go through it.

The insights she has gained over the last thirty years of her sobriety and the inner work she did as a result of confronting her alcoholism have carried over to "outside" experiences of impasse. Naming the impasse, recognizing that she cannot control the situation or another person's behavior, rank high on the list of learnings. Acknowledging and accepting the wisdom and support of others, while remaining truthful to the struggle and faithful to prayer, are important tools that have helped her face other experiences of impasse. Making the connections, learning from past experiences, now helps her ask, "How am I contributing to the impasse? In what way or ways am I consciously or unconsciously a part of the destructive or unjust situation? What does this impasse tell me about my expectations, desires, and needs?" Asking ourselves these and similar questions as we face situations of impasse might help us center ourselves better and find positive and creative new ways to respond.

I have come to understand the power of open-ended questions. To engage impasse is a scary and difficult process. It tests our perseverance and ability to acknowledge our own vulnerability. Impasse creates tension and reactions based on a variety of feelings: fear, insecurity, shame. Our emotions and feelings come in many different shapes and sizes. What might cause anger or disappointment in one person, does not necessarily provoke the same emotion in another.

The Design Team offered us a process to explore our feelings about engaging impasse, inviting us to ask ourselves, "As I reflect on my experience of impasse, what do I feel?" After we identified a feeling, we then asked ourselves, "Why does this experience make me feel this way?" Whatever answer we came up with, we then asked again: "Why does my answer make me feel this way?" We repeated this "why" question five times; each new answer brought us closer to exposing the root cause of our feelings. When one of the theologians in our small circle responded to these questions, her answers touched me deeply. She feared being silenced. She feared losing her teaching position at a Catholic university. This fear caused her to wonder if her congregation would experience any repercussions. Would they be held hostage while the ecclesial authorities questioned her writings and/or teachings? Since her vocation to be a theologian is as much a part of her identity as her vocation to be a woman religious, she wondered what the repercussions would be for her future. As she pondered the ramifications of a very possible situation, she said, "I also wonder if anyone would stand with me. And if they did, what would that look like?" Her vulnerability and open-ended ponderings raised questions about my own responsibility. What would I do if this were to happen?

One inch long. Many miles deep. Now all this sounds fine, but you and I know that transformative work doesn't just happen. It takes consistent discipline and periodic renewal experiences. It is here that my Dominican vocation has been indelibly strengthened.

To celebrate this gift of renewal, each morning, before I sit quietly in prayer, I light the votive candle, "She Who Watches,"[18] to remind me that I do not sit alone. As "She Who Watches" sits with me, lighting the darkness before dawn, she reminds me that "the darkness embraces everything; creatures and me, people and nations—just as they are."[19] There is nothing to fear in the presence of this Holy One. She reminds me that the Divine dwells within me and that I am surrounded by Holy Mystery. Her watchful stance also assures me that all those She has looked upon vigil with me.

I am strengthened by knowing that each of the circle women sits with me, listening from her own landscape some time during the day. In the shadows of the morning, I see their faces—my circle friends—along with the faces of many other seekers who have dug deep searching for truth. In the silence I hear their voices along with other ancient whisperings of Wisdom that sound a ring of warning and promise: "The breeze at dawn has secrets to tell. Don't go back to sleep. You must ask for what you really want. Don't go back to sleep."[20] As I pray for them, I know, too, that I am re-membered in this circle company of holy women.

I feel renewed. As a preacher, daily I attentively examine our ancestors' stories in the Bible to draw new insights from these ancient parables, poetry, and other writings. For me, this Story is never out-of-date or irrelevant; when brought into our times, it is a story as fresh as the spring daffodils in my garden and the wild flowers that press through the soggy spring knolls on the California hillsides of the Napa valley. It is as reliable as the sunset on the San Francisco Bay or the return of the monogamous mourning doves that care for their spring families in our fig tree. It is as startling as the howl of a wolf in the clear night air announcing the birth of its young. And yes, even in the midst of these spring events, the Story also holds the memory of our inevitable winters. Winter is as cyclical as spring. Its long dark nights are as real as the isolation they can bring.

I find hope and healing in the natural world around me. Walking along the Headlands near Sausalito, I'm poignantly aware of God's noisy, attractive presence in the ocean's breaking waves. Hiking through the reverent redwood forest of Muir Woods, I am astounded at the beauty and strength of old age. Meister Eckardt's words echo in the hollow of my being, "Every creature is a word of God."[21]

I know, too, that the circle gatherings were more than a way to make new friends, even though that has happened. I know they were more than the stories of poignant joys, sorrows, disappointments, and accomplishments. I know that when we heard each other's voices in conversation, we heard more clearly the Other's voice in contemplation. I know that our shared "sittings" were much more than the silence or verbal prayers that followed. I know God gathered us together in a unique way to do something new. It was in this company of wise women that God would do God's work even though I/we may not yet perceive its fullness.

Patricia Bruno, OP is a Promoter of Preaching for the Dominican Sisters of San Rafael and the Regional Promoter for the Western Province in the USA. She is a member of the board of the Academy of Preachers and the National Dominican Preaching Team and directs retreats and parish renewals. She has worked in economic justice education and has co-authored a workbook, titled FROM VIOLENCE TO WHOLENESS.

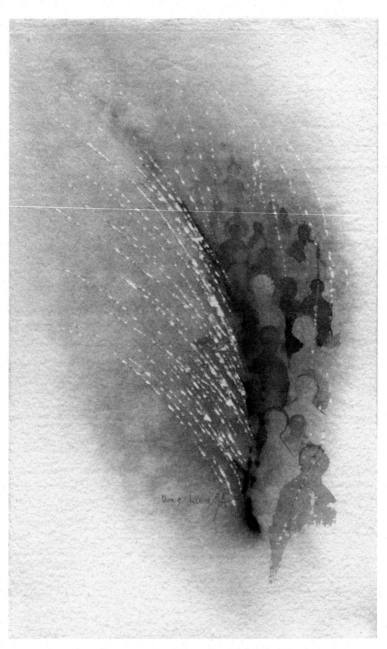

Courage To Cross the Threshold

Becoming the Change We Want To See

Joellen McCarthy, BVM; Peggy Nolan, BVM;
and Mary Ann Zollmann, BVM

Three weeks into our term as the new leadership team of the Sisters of Charity of the Blessed Virgin Mary, we stood with a thousand other women religious in the convention center in Albuquerque and applauded Nancy Sylvester, IHM at the conclusion of her 2000 Leadership Conference of Women Religious (LCWR) address, "Everything Before Us Brought Us to This Moment, Standing on the Threshold of a Brand New Day."[22]

As women religious, to hear our situation of impasse in relation to the institutional Church proclaimed publicly was both exhilarating and heartrending. To stand shoulder-to-shoulder with so many and know that we are not alone filled us with amazing gratitude, affection, and hope. How freeing to hear the truth of our experiences of ecclesial oppression named aloud. How powerful to claim that truth with others. As we look back on the last four years, and in particular on the way our participation in the *Engaging Impasse* circles has affected us as a leadership team, this powerful image of liberation and solidarity has continued to inspire us.

We were led to participate in the circles by several factors, including two foundational beliefs that have shaped our leadership style.

We believed in the power of mutual relationships. We believed that creating such relationships—among the three of us as team; among congregational members, committees and regions; and among those with whom we interacted outside the congregation—was of primary importance.

We held the conviction that what happens in a given situation arises out of how it happens. Desiring to understand how things happen has pushed us in our exercise of leadership to explore the processes underlying situations and events within our congregation, Church, and world.

Both beliefs are grounded in our deep faith in a God whose power is shared and whose divine energy continually seeks to draw us together in relationships of mutuality.

In addition to these foundational beliefs, at least two other factors led us to participate in the *Engaging Impasse* circles. Mary Ann's election to the LCWR presidency in August 2001 meant that three of our four years in leadership would be marked by her intense involvement with the national leadership issues of the Conference. Because of this, we have explored the complex issue of women in relation to the institutional Church more than we might have otherwise.

Ongoing study also led us to the circles. In our first year in leadership, we attended monthly sessions on "Family Systems"[23] where we explored our families of origin, our congregation as an emotional system, and the effect of behaviors learned in our families on the way we exercise leadership. We learned the pivotal importance of claiming responsibility for our beliefs and behaviors as leaders, thus freeing both leadership and the organization to function with greater emotional health. In the second year of our leadership, we gathered with a group of local BVMs to probe the writings of Brazilian theologian Ivone Gebara. This process of reading, reflection, and dialogue sharpened our critical thinking skills, and invited us to imagine ways our Christian faith might honor the experience of the marginalized, particularly women.

In February 2002, Joellen and Peggy attended a meeting of the LCWR Systemic Change Think Tank in Florida and once again met Nancy Sylvester. Nancy was wondering who might be interested in joining other women to focus contemplatively on their experience of impasse with the institutional Church or with societal structures. Intrigued by the possibility, Joellen and Peggy came home and said to Mary Ann, "What about it?" We knew the answer immediately, and amazingly our schedules cooperated.

The sense of "everything before us brought us to this moment" was amplified and expanded in our experience of the *Engaging Impasse* circles.

A LINGERING UNSETTLEDNESS IN TELLING OUR STORY

The first circle gathering found us in a group of fourteen women religious leaders telling each other our stories of impasse with the institutional Church. They were stories of feeling dismissed, excluded, discounted, and devalued by bishops who think nuns are no longer a group with whom they need to deal; they were stories of feeling isolated and alone in speaking the truth of our perspective as we try to honor the women, the history, the legacy of our congregations; they were stories of feeling paralyzed when the complexity of issues is met with simplistic solutions and silencing.

Our own story took place in the fall of 2001. As a leadership team, we had made the decision to host a New Ways Ministry Workshop at our motherhouse.[24] We subsequently informed our bishop as a matter of courtesy, only to realize that he could not support our decision. The conversation that ensued highlighted our differing understandings of New Ways Ministry's pastoral approaches to homosexuality, as well as our differing interpretations of sexual ethics. These conversations positioned us in the painful tension between wanting to be true to ourselves and yet stay in relationship with our bishop.

In the dialogue, we were led to a place of compromise. Honoring his episcopal position as guardian of faith-teaching in the archdiocese, we agreed to not open our workshop to diocesan pastoral ministers, but to keep the workshop at the motherhouse as an educational venture for our sisters. Honoring the ministry of New Ways, we assisted in the relocation of a second, and public, workshop to a neutral place in our town. In this situation we tried to speak our truth as women, to bring many sides of a conversation forward, and to continue to be present with and speak on behalf of those who are marginalized within our Church.

As we told this story, we were aware of a lingering unsettledness; the compromise had pushed us to question our ability to live in the fullness of our integrity and at the same time live in right relationship with ecclesial authority. Disturbing though it is, this ongoing questioning provides fresh opportunities for further reflection and dialogue.

In telling our own story and hearing the stories of others in the circles, we experienced profoundly the power of mutual relationship and felt the bond of solidarity created by the shared vulnerability of our situations. While the three of us might doubt our own experience, the integrity, competency, and deep spirituality of our companions in the circle were completely credible. Together we could own our experience as real and significant, worthy of being probed further for its revelation to us. We could claim this story as "the Word of God broken open these days,"echoing the words of our closing ritual.

FROM VICTIMIZATION TO COMPLICITY TO RECLAIMING POWER

In the second circle gathering, held six months later, we moved from the pain of victimization by patriarchal and hierarchical structures, to the pain of recognizing our own complicity in impasse. We named our complicity in situations where we kept silent for fear of consequences. For example, in the New Ways Ministry situation described above, we did not want our relationship with our bishop to be so ruptured that it would negatively affect our dealings with him in the future. We also admitted that we, as educated women of privilege, have used our power to control others. In this second session, we began to experience how the practices of contemplation and contemplative dialogue help us see our part in creating the impasse, and then help move us beyond the complicity of either acquiescence or domination to a transformed way of seeing, being, and acting.

In each of the circle gatherings we sat together in silence for considerable periods of time, taking a long loving look at the feelings, images, and symbols that arose within us. In the second gathering, especially, we noticed that symbols arising from the silence opened us to paradox, leading us to surprising places. Mary Ann described herself as being on an elevator. As the elevator descended, the light grew dimmer until finally the elevator stopped in total darkness. Sitting there in the darkness, Mary Ann realized that the darkness of impasse was caused not just by structures and systems of oppression by others; by remaining silent in unjust situations, she was being complicit with oppressive systems. In her prevailing attitude of victimization, she was surrendering her power to the powers of injustice.

> By remaining silent in unjust situations, she was surrendering her power to the powers of injustice.

Staying with the surprise and *pain* of this recognition, Mary Ann claimed her power to be an agent of change by speaking her truth and by opening up to the creative possibilities inherent in her position on the margins of official ecclesial structures. As Mary Ann sensed the liberation of this powerful insight, she felt the elevator begin to ascend and saw the darkness begin to fade. Experiences like this one, which emerged in the stillness and silence of communal contemplation, helped us acknowledge our complicity in impasse and to practice ways of relating that would help our Church and world move beyond both the arrogance and subservience upon which systems and structures of patriarchy and hierarchy depend.

PRACTICING CONTEMPLATIVE DIALOGUE

In this second gathering, we were also introduced to the practice of contemplative dialogue, a way of listening and conversing characterized by slowness of pace and openness to whatever insight might emerge from the group. Contemplative dialogue took to a deeper level our earlier team strategies of creating mutual relationships. In contemplative dialogue we learned to follow the flow of the conversation rather than trying to control its direction by inserting our own thoughts, to listen underneath the surface of what was being said, to concentrate on what the other was offering rather than on what we were hoping to say, and to speak only after having carefully considered if one's contribution would contribute something unique to the dialogue.

In practicing contemplative dialogue, we realized that what was emerging did not depend solely upon any one of us, nor could it have come to visibility without any one of us. This practice was moving us beyond the complicity of acquiescence where we give our power to another, and moving us beyond the complicity of domination where we take power away from others. In surrendering to the rhythm of the conversa-

> In surrendering to the rhythm of the conversation, we experienced the power of true mutuality that is both receptive to the other and active in the speaking of one's own distinct truth.

tion, we experienced the power of true mutuality that is both receptive to the other and active in the speaking of one's own distinct truth.

LIVING FROM THE WILD SPACES

Six months later we arrived at our third and final circle gathering, unsure of what to expect. When we began almost a year earlier we wondered—given the nature of the impasses identified—if at the end we would be in rebellion against the institution or in despair over our situation. Neither proved to be true. In the final gathering, our engaging of impasse led us to a sense of being on the edge of something, on the margins. This is not a place of feeling discarded, dismissed, or abandoned. Rather it is a place of freedom and spaciousness that allows us to engage impasse in a new way.

Symbols emerged for us that reveal the freedom and spaciousness we experienced. The packet of wildflower seeds that we had received at the end of the second gathering became a symbol for the wildness that gives us freedom and space. If these seeds remain in their bag, they contribute nothing to the life around them. If we domesticate the unique wildness of our individual lives, a dimension of creation is forever lost. Participating in these circle gatherings awakened us to the value of not "fitting in" to the Church and society around us. Living from the wild spaces allows God to break out of our boundaries and to beckon us beyond our safe places. The wildflower symbolizes a way of living that engages with its surroundings without becoming enmeshed. It has no need to fit in. This freedom to claim our wildness provides the space to stand tall in our own stories. From the vantage point of the margin, our responsibility is not so much to change the world or the Church directly, but to claim our story and tell it out loud.

During the final gathering we considered the question, *"What is dawning in us about impasse?"* At dawn, we experience most keenly the leaning of Earth toward its magnificent source of energy, our sun. Standing on the surface of Earth we are invited to wake up to the innate power of the universe moving us toward life, and to draw upon the wisdom of the cosmos moving us toward new strategies for engaging impasse. The "new cosmology"—the story we humans are coming to learn about the origin and 13.7-billion-year evolutionary unfolding of the universe and our role in it—has become our teacher. We learn from the universe that diversity strengthens not weakens unity; that life and death are not a duality but aspects of one mystery; that everything in creation is distinct from but related to everything else; that humans are not separate from nor in control of nature's processes,

> We learn from the universe that diversity strengthens, not weakens, unity.

but are intertwined with them in such a way as to make domination of any kind unthinkable.

Many people are beginning to experience a shift of consciousness by stepping into the flow of life heralded by the new cosmology. Standing in this flow requires giving up control of outcomes and claiming one's own identity. When those engaging in this process reach a critical mass, change occurs, change that will affect the Church and the world. In the *Engaging Impasse* circles we recognized ourselves as part of this huge transformation of consciousness.

In the ritual of this third gathering we made our own candles from loose wax pieces, signaling the value of unifying the fragments of our lives. We recognized that the total participation of the group throughout the three gatherings was gathered up in these fragments and the stuff of each of our lives had truly contributed to the shaping of the new consciousness we were experiencing. As a congregational leadership team we saw how insights from our earlier study were reinforced throughout the circle gatherings, particularly the exhilaration of naming our truth, and the joy of being in solidarity. Choosing to meet challenging situations not with reactivity but with new strategies harkened back to our Family Systems sessions: speak your truth; and in so doing, don't attack, don't defend, don't withdraw.

ENGAGING IMPASSE AT HOME

As we look back on the time before, during, and after our participation in the *Engaging Impasse* circles, we ask ourselves what difference has it made that we participated? Where can we see in our work as leaders that anything has really changed? In trying to answer this question for ourselves, we chose one situation, seeking clues that we had responded differently and that the difference could be traced to our work in the circles. The situation we have chosen to describe is our own congregational reality regarding tensions around the meaning and celebration of Eucharist.

In exploring this topic with our members we used the experience of the *Engaging Impasse* circles as a reference point. At last summer's congregational assembly, we described the connection between our participation in the gatherings and our congregational tension around Eucharist in this way:

> *We have joined other women religious leaders in participating in a series of gatherings, called "Engaging Impasse." These gatherings respond to an issue LCWR has been addressing for a number of years regarding a pattern of abuse in the exercise of ecclesial authority within the institutional Church. Because of our close identification with the Church, this pattern is felt keenly by women religious, but is also the experience of many women and men. Years of dealing with this issue result in a sense of powerlessness and disconnection known as impasse. In the experience of impasse, not only women religious, but also other women and some men in the Christian community, find themselves:*
>
> • *Excluded from significant decision-making processes at most levels of our Church;*
> • *Expected to follow ethics that they have been prohibited from shaping;*

• Left out of or offended by some of the language used in worship and doctrine;

• Offered mainly masculine images of God;

• Prohibited from breaking open the word and blessing the bread in liturgical settings.

Living with a sense of impasse in relationship to the institutional Church challenges us individually and congregationally as we seek to participate in Church. As a BVM congregation we experience the impasse around Church most immediately in our struggle to celebrate the Eucharist together.

Having learned from the gatherings the value of telling the story of our experience, we went on in our address to describe as fully as we could the pain that we are experiencing with one another regarding this topic. "Despite our best efforts, we find ourselves not at home as we approach the Eucharistic banquet together. ... For many of us cherished beliefs about Eucharist co-exist with a haunting awareness of patterns of ecclesial exclusion."

Our Family Systems work had taught us as leaders the primary importance of defining our own position on an issue, thus creating space for others to do likewise. We knew that as a leadership team our chief concern about Eucharist was not so much the content of what sisters individually believe and practice, but the quality of their interaction with each other. For us, staying in relationship was and is at the heart of this issue. And so in our talk we noted that, "The depth of our pain over Eucharist is a testament to our care for one another in community." If we didn't care for each other so much, it wouldn't matter to us so deeply. Having learned from the *Engaging Impasse* circles the value of being vulnerable, of acknowledging our own complicity in the pain we experience, and of staying with the pain, we believed that the best way to approach our tension around Eucharist was from a stance of vulnerability.

Thus, in our talk we encouraged our sisters to see this place of great discomfort as a place of both suffering and hope. We called each other "to practice nonviolence in our attitudes, behaviors, and conversations." Aware that our actions in one area influence other related areas, we said, "The choice to share our power with one another through honest dialogue, sincere reflection and persistent prayer provides an alternative to the pattern of abuse in the exercise of power to which we have grown accustomed in both the Church and world." Our vulnerable and respectful listening to one another in this place of tension could be a powerful force for change beyond our own small world.

Recognizing from the *Engaging Impasse* circles the power of the imagination to move us to new places, we encouraged one another to imagine:

- a Church that includes both genders in significant decision-making processes;
- ethics that are shaped by the experiences of all people;
- a language of worship and doctrine that leaves no one out;
- an array of images of God; and
- a Church that welcomes fully the gifts and talents of both women and men.

While the situation of impasse around Eucharist continues within our community, many sisters are sharing with each other their personal experiences and beliefs about Eucharist. In this process they are attending to the vulnerability in themselves and in one another, they are laying down defenses and still feeling safe, and they are coming to understand more readily the different perspectives they find.

In this unfolding situation of tension around Eucharist in our congregation, we are grateful for the experience of the *Engaging Impasse* circles. We believe that staying present to each other in the impasse, naming our respective truths, acknowledging our own complicity in creating the situation, honoring the differences among us, and practicing contemplation and contemplative dialogue will lead us to a place of greater spaciousness and freedom. As leaders who are personally committed to the above strategies, we take to heart Gandhi's challenge, "To be the change we want to see."[25] We continue to believe that "everything before us brought us to this moment." Thanks to the impact of the *Engaging Impasse* circles we have fresh courage to cross the threshold into a brand new day.

Joellen McCarthy (right) is president of the Sisters of Charity of the Blessed Virgin Mary. Previously, she coordinated orientation for the Maryknoll Lay Missioners and served as a teacher, parish minister, member of the BVM Formation Team, and missionary in León, Nicaragua.

Peggy Nolan (middle) serves as vice-president of the BVMs. Her earlier ministries include regional leadership in Chicago, high school teaching, parish ministry, work on the BVM Formation Team, and serving on the staff of the Working Boys Center in Quito, Ecuador.

Mary Ann Zollmann (left), 2002 President of LCWR, is vice-president of the BVMs. Formerly she was a professor of religious studies and campus minister at Clarke College in Dubuque, Iowa. She also coordinated the BVM Initial Membership program and served as a secondary school teacher.

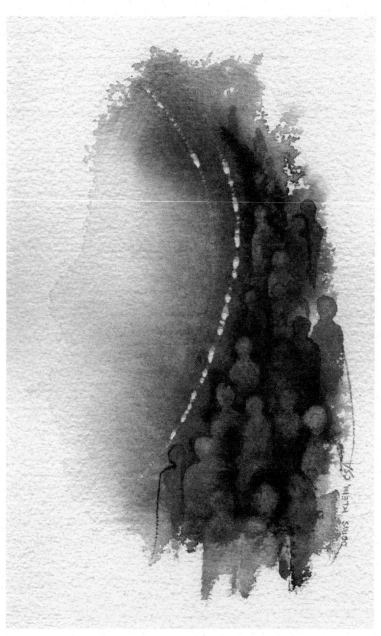

Willing Hearts To Journey Together

Resisting the Isolating Allure of Impasse
Simone Campbell, SSS

I was wrong. Let me just state it boldly—I was very wrong! Writing of the experience of engaging impasse is not the easy task that I thought it would be. The truth of the experience slips from my grasp every time I try to approach it directly. How does one person write of a communal reality? It becomes a personal impasse of sorts. So let me try, as we did in the process, to set the scene with a personal sharing of a story—a brief synopsis of one view of my spiritual journey, followed then by impasse, and engaging. I write in the first person not in certitude, but in personal puzzlement. This is not a road map, but a wandering and a wondering.

SHARING THE CONTEXT

I came to the *Engaging Impasse* process with a twenty-year history of a Christian Zen practice. It is the heart of how I am spiritual, and has manifested itself in a variety of ways:

• In the beginning of my Zen practice (which I refer to as "sitting"), my work as an attorney became rooted in opening my heart to my clients. In the process I discovered that their need and struggle nourished me. It was food for the journey, and in the process I came to know "multi-sided partiality", *i.e.*, caring about a variety of perspectives at the same time.

• Then I was elected to the crucible of leadership in our religious community during a very difficult time. (We had just lost our motherhouse in the 1994 Northridge Earthquake—creating metaphorical and actual aftershocks.) In this context I found the direct and implied criticism of me by community members challenging to bear. So I came to sit with the criticism that hurt me until I knew the truth of that criticism. One example of this was sitting with the criticism that I was "not a spiritual leader—I was too corporate." The truth that I came to know was that I was spiritual, but I had not shown this part of myself to my sisters. They had only seen the corporate side—so I was called to speak more directly from my spiritual core. Thus, once I knew the truth of a criticism, I was freed from the barb, gained insight into myself and did not close myself to my sisters. (It sounds so simple when I write this—but know it was an anguished, gifted process.)

• During a sabbatical following the five years of leadership, I spent six weeks in a Zen residency program where I learned several things: the only piece I bring to the contemplative life is a willing heart; a contemplative experience is shut down by fear and grasping;[26] to be "lost" in God requires being stripped of my illusions about myself.[27] I experienced God as the hum that holds all of creation together all the time. In this process I came to express myself as a poet; I am still a puppy poet (terribly enthusiastic, but not quite house broken)!

• Post sabbatical I took a job as the director of a statewide California interfaith social justice lobby. I have tried to lobby from a contemplative stance—not righteous but open to the truth of all. I come willing to share my heart with legislators and lobby-ists and ask that they do the same. But it is very challenging to walk this path where contemplation is in the relationships of daily life and not just on my meditation cushion in the morning. During the day I would often rather be right than open. But I am caught in a profound experience of the divine that changes everything. I can't do business as usual, but have no vocabulary or way of thinking about it differently. All I can say is:

I yearn to practice
a mysticism that meets,
moves, mobilizes a piece of
the mundane world.
I hunger to use my gifts
of poetry and practicality,
of language and law to engage
part of the achy world.

My harness of Peter-ish
impetuosity matters not

at all, for I am hobbled
by blindness.

Please, use this moment
of light luminous
dark in time or no time
to reveal the next step.

I came to our circle on societal impasse eager for a next step. There I found seven other women of different backgrounds, all with willing hearts to journey together. We groped our way to connection through risk, laughter, yoga, dance, embracing the time and each other. In the process I/we began to develop a vocabulary and some sharing of metaphors that allowed for exploration. How bold to talk out loud about the contemplative journey!

We were to bring a story of impasse to the first gathering. Interestingly, even though we were in turbulent times in our society and only two weeks away from the 2003 invasion of Iraq, the stories we shared were all personal in some way. Mine was the story of having been in Iraq three months earlier (December 2002) and having unknowingly hardened my heart to the children. I expressed my experience in the following:

Winter of Redemption

Dusty childhood rote might lead to revealing this piece
of sin and come perhaps to sacramental healing.
The mantra allows for circling to the core of hidden
truths, performing childhood ritual comforts, managing
a painful view of failing—Bless me fathers, mothers,

sisters, brothers, for I have sinned. It has been
far too long since my last confession,
and this is my frightful sin—a sin that looked like
openness and easy going empathy; but let me
declare to you the well masked sin—a sin of hiding.

I hid in hallways, I hid in schedules, toys, photos,
other distancing realities to protect my heart from
failure writ Imax large before my eyes. In the face
of war's threat, I cowered, pulled in upon my stoic
self, sealed my being as I'd been taught in nurtured
nature protection. I hear often eager responses to
quell, quiet this awkward revelation. It is said—
"This is human, nothing more. We share this plight,
hiding in toil and tasks." Ah, but such comfort negates
my human hunger to confess with painful
personal precession my particular frail fault:

In the face of threatened Mideast violence, rattled war,
I hid from Iraqi children's laughter and their need.
I lacked the courage to touch their trust, the purity
to hold their innocence. Lacking songs of safety, poetry
of promise, I could not safe guard these little ones
from war's pernicious threat. And this the
weak-kneed truth, I hid my hiding from myself
until safely away from nursery, preschool
orphanage, church, mosque. While I wept

with grown ups, with rumors of war and promised
grief, I was sealed from the children's worried
laughter. Trying to open to it now I find only
silence, an empty void. I sit before this failing,
wait for revelation, healing or just forgiveness.

*I wait for a penance to atone for such heart
hardness. Please give me a penance to ease this
burden. Please give me sight to meet the children's
eyes. Please give me a path to peace.*

As I shared and reflected on this impasse and embraced the impasses of my "circle-mates," I came to the following reflections.

THE "FEAR AND GRASPING" OF IMPASSE

Impasse is a visceral experience—which has cerebral parts. We often spoke of impasse using the gesture of two fists pushing against each other. There was force, pressure, and the gut-wrenching sense of being locked in a struggle. It also seemed to be facing a blank wall, not knowing the way through to resolution. In the conversation it was analytically discussed as an "out there" reality. And then we had a conflict in the group—a misunderstanding, a sense of judging and being judged, the inevitable rub of perceptions and personality. What a breathtaking moment that was in our nice little secure nest! I have forgotten the details of tension, but it shook our easygoing relationships. The main protagonists chose to deal with it in the group without realizing at the time that it was impasse. So holding our breath we explored the reality of unexpected difference.

In Myers-Briggs terms, I am a "T" (thinker). I manage fear (like of earthquakes—metaphorical and actual) by treating things as science and data gathering. But this conflict of personal relationships yanked me to the visceral level where minds and thought do not rule. Rather we walked together into a struggle and explored. Ironically, as much as we resisted this exploration, once engaged, it gave birth to a greater intimacy in the group.

This led me to a possible second insight: Impasse is the product of fear and grasping. Now because I am called to live a contemplative life (which is all the time), I need to remember that "fear and grasping" will shut down the contemplative experience, á la Transfiguration.[28] There, Peter in one moment wants to pitch a tent and stay in the experience of the transcendent and in the next is quivering, huddled in fear. So I am beginning to think the essence of impasse is just that—fear and grasping. I am often afraid that I will be changed in ways that I do not want to be and so hold on to myself, my old ways. I fear that if I open myself to the reality of another (especially neo-conservatives), I will be swamped, lost, adrift. So I hold on to my perspective and do not listen.

In our circle's exploration I came to think: Impasse is the result of dichotomous thinking. It is the "either/or" reality that sets up the struggle in me. I have a strong Greco-American (or human?) desire to be right, win, succeed. I like winning a case, succeeding in lobbying an issue, having my view triumph. But I have come to know that this very desire is like the biblical story of Adam and Eve in the Garden. The snake was right: when we do experience the fruits of the tree of the knowledge of good and evil we make ourselves "like God" judging what is "good" and "bad," what I let in and what I do not. The process of judgment sets me apart from other creatures and I gain a sense of isolated self and lose the communal reality.[29]

So if impasse has an isolating allure, what might encourage us to engage? I have a hunch that the basic reality is that the hunger for community and communing draws us in—hopefully with greater force than the comforting lure of isolation, or the self-protecting response of fear and grasping. But what are the elements of this experience of engaging?

> If impasse has an isolating allure, what might encourage us to engage?

First of all, I think a struggle from my last retreat is appropriate here. To go this journey, I need to sit as comfortably with chaos as with clarity! This is a very big challenge for a person who likes to organize, to have a plan, and to know the intended result. But my experience of trying to be true to the contemplative journey is to engage ambiguity and live in the dark. If I am not the measure of accomplishment (in other words—if I am not God), then I do not have the full plan, perspective, etc.; I can only do my part. I need to sit in life with my partial view, my common darkness, and not treat it as clarity or certainty. I have come to realize that chaos or darkness can be nurturing. I like the image of the murk of the ocean and the fact that the cold waters can be so dense because they are filled with plankton and nutrients. The Caribbean's clarity is the result of there being little nourishment in the water. It is in fact an ocean desert. My experience is that engaging this contemplative journey is much more akin to the cold murky northern Pacific than the crystal clear Caribbean.

In this context, the process of engagement of impasse means: we do not have a clue about the results. In my experience, it means dealing with life as it is presented. For me the contemplative path is more about attitude and stance in the world than about strategic plans. I must confess that this perspective might be more a reflection of the fact that I have lived my almost forty years of religious life in a community dedicated to the Holy Spirit. We are engaged in social mission and come at things from a social-work intuitive perspective. So maybe I am more open to process than content—even though I still love to have a sense of results. But it does seem to be a key to my experience of the contemplative process to not have expectations about the "end point" or a "result." I have always been surprised.

To be open to surprises requires that I slow down enough to notice more than my own thoughts and opinions. For me it means letting go of not only results, but also a "deadline." When I can be detached from my timeline, I am freer to explore and to trust the other person and the process.

...I have a hunch that the basic reality is that the hunger for community and communing draws us in.

This open stance is framed for me first in asking curious questions about another person. This is key to opening my heart to that person and to opening my eyes to another point of view. I realize that I start by trying to "sit" with the question of "What next?" while holding legislators, lobbyists—as well as my own daily life—in care-filled concern. This challenges me while I am advocating for healthcare, and a Republican dismisses my proposals as "job killers" that will scuttle the economy and hurt more Californians. I have come to sit with this reality and try to be led by en-Spirited insights—always a challenge. This has led me to ask questions of legislators: "How can we as a society care for the 'least among us?'" It seems that by assuming that the other possesses a good heart, cares, and wants to respond to the needs of others, there is a way of meeting beyond ideology. What it has required in me is the willingness to risk being interested in the answer. I need to move beyond my preconceptions, unclench my fists, acknowledge my fear and grasping, and let go of my desire to win and have my idea prevail. I need to risk moving in the dark in uncharted territory.

> I need to let go of my desire to win and have my idea prevail.

A second element of this open stance is having enough trust to be willing to speak of spiritual realities. For me, this does not mean speaking of religion; rather it means being willing to explore together the spiritual questions as I journey and invite others to join me. I used to be very shy about doing that and generally have an allergic reaction to "religious talk." I now find myself in situations that seem to call for that level of conversation. At JERICHO, a statewide California interfaith social justice lobby, we started the "Sister Prayer Project." We recruited about 140 Catholic sisters (mostly retired) from around the state who have committed to pray for an assigned legislator and the legislator's staff and family every day. The sisters received the photo and biography of the legislator. I then met with the legislators and gave them the photo and biography of the sister. What happened often was a shift in conversation that brought the issues of faith, values, and personal struggles, into the conversation. It also began to create relationships that are beyond ideology, maybe because it presumed trust.

In this context of presumed trust and risk-taking beyond personal boundaries, our circle began to develop vocabulary to speak with new metaphors for what we had imaged as impasse. We came to speak of being a river that can surround boulders that are in the way (formerly seen as impasses). As a river, we knew that we could not be "broken" by rocks. Faithfulness calls for fluidity. We imagined that we might be the moon—radiating light in different phases, but not being the light itself. We spoke of "surrendering my Grand Plan." And we expressed a hunger to "live from the inside out."

Now, Trusting the Beauty of Chaos

As a result of this process, I have been confirmed in this journey—I really cannot do it in another way. I still mourn my hardhearted response in Iraq. I do not know what it means to be a "contemplative lobbyist." But the lack of resolution and the lack of clarity bother me less. I am choosing to keep up the discipline of sitting in the mornings and to ask curious questions. I still have preferences and resistances that I wrestle with, but I trust that all things work to the good—even if I don't understand them. I live in the dark, trust in the beauty of chaos, and pray daily that I might be the moon for others—even if I don't know it. Finally, I give thanks for my resistances—they are the edge of my redemption.

Living Waters

Impetuous me favors the passionate tumult of Spring river flooding. Sensuous me favors the indolent caress of Summer river flowing. Reflective me favors the penetrating seep of Autumn river trickling. Even aloof shy me favors the chilled reserve of Winter river freezing. But, all of me resists evaporation.

I resist the sucking pulling warm air wresting me from known boundaries. I resist drifting unseen to unknown parts. I resist the uncertainty of unformed floating yearning rather to surround rocks, carve new paths. I resist the ambiguous foggy drift. But luckily, at times, I am yanked into air. There

beholding earth's impasses: Weep! Weeping, raining, puddling…perhaps the beginning of an exuberant Spring.

Simone Campbell, a Sister of Social Service, recently completed service as the executive director of JERICHO (an interfaith pub-

lic policy and advocacy organization) where she lobbied for the needs of those who live at the economic margins in the State of California. She now serves as National Coordinator of NETWORK, a national Catholic social justice lobby based in Washington, D.C. Simone has eighteen years of experience as an attorney for the working poor in Oakland, California, and five years as the leader of her international community. She enjoys the experience of other cultures, speaking Spanish, and traveling to distant parts.

Impasse: Birthing Creativity

Be-ing in the Story

Margaret Galiardi, OP and Rose Mary Meyer, BVM

Margaret: You and I come from very different backgrounds. You were raised on a farm in Missouri and I in the suburbs of New York City. In spite of this difference, we both found ourselves reflecting on impasse in the context of the larger 13.7-billion-year-old "Universe Story." How did you come to this?

Rose Mary: My early roots were in the rich, fertile, black soil of northwest Missouri farmland. This fertile soil and the brilliant vastness of the Milky Way in the night sky provided the context for my first understanding of God. This was one of God as everywhere, a connecting, creating presence. I remember asking my father when I was a young child if the people in China also saw the Milky Way. He assured me that they did. I immediately felt connected to them and delighted that they too enjoy this gift. As my father and I stood outside and watched the artistry of the Northern Lights, I felt awe, gratitude, connection, and joy at the spectacular diversity. Something happened to me though, when the local country school closed. I had to walk to catch a bus to attend school in town. There at the bus stop on the dirt road were other young rural children, some of whom, in the midst of winter, had shoes with loose flopping soles and worn-thin sweaters. I remember wondering why some children did not have enough winter clothes and others had an abundance of them. Economic inequities seared my consciousness early in life.

The living embers of that early-life searing flared up in the experience of impasse I shared at our first circle gathering. It involved a decision to end the life of a national organization that had facilitated opportunities for diverse women, locally, regionally, and internationally, to share experiences and to struggle actively for gender equity in both Church and society. The organization's newsletter and educational materials documented the women's stories and struggles for justice. The harshness of the economic reality of no longer being able to meet financial commitments was a justice issue involving staff and other people. In spite of the dynamism of the organization, the impasse of inadequate financial resources caused the closure. As a board member of the organization, I experienced the decision as pain-full. To acknowledge the grief connected with this loss, two of us created a ritual to honor the friendships, the justice actions, the connectedness reaching beyond organizational boundaries. This ritualizing deepened my awareness of the unfolding interconnectivity of the spirit of the organization, which extends beyond the closure. I realize now that the vision of justice lives on in the hearts of women everywhere who are still struggling to change unjust systems in order to achieve gender equity. These women are light to themselves and to others, as are the stars in the Milky Way.

What about you Margaret, what brought you to this reflection?

Margaret: Ironically, it was an experience of impasse that led me to the universe story, so it makes sense that my reflections on impasse are grounded in a 13-billion-year perspective. I came to the circles with great hope and excitement. From the first moment that Connie FitzGerald's writings fell into my hands in the early 1980s, they struck a deep chord within me. I was working at the time at the Intercommunity Center for Justice and Peace in Manhattan. FitzGerald's article, "Impasse and Dark Night," offered a new lens through which to view the Reagan years. For sure, "we could find no escape from the world we [had] built, where the poor and oppressed cry out, where the earth and the environment cry out, and where the specter of nuclear waste...haunts future generations."[30] It was FitzGerald's work perhaps more than anything else that encouraged me to continue the search for "a new and integrating spirituality capable of creating a new politics and generating new social structures."[31] The pursuit of this desire was to throw me into an impasse where I would stand helplessly on the precipice of what felt like despair, wondering just what I could do about anything. From that spot I would learn about gifts, which, in FitzGerald's words, "catch and bind the falling desperate person to God."[32]

Rose Mary: It sounds as if your work at the Center led you into impasse and shaped your thinking about it.

Margaret: Yes. The more I was involved in trying to effect structural change, the more I came to the stark conviction that even the most creative and radical of strategies to effect change yielded what felt to me like a kind of "damage control." That was very necessary, but it still left us far from the desired outcome. Trying to get to the root of the problem led me to a period of sustained reflection on the work of Thomas Berry, Brian Swimme and sister Dominican, Miriam Therese McGillis, OP. Their work pointed out what seemed to me to be "the fatal flaw" of the dominant societal and ecclesial institutions: a radical discontinuity with Earth. While maintaining a profound respect for the variety of approaches to effect the change so earnestly sought by many, I felt I wanted and needed to be about building alternatives grounded in the insights gained from reflecting on the origin and ongoing unfolding of the universe, and the role of the human in that unfolding. I gave expression to all of this when I wrote in the biography we had to prepare for our first circle gathering: "For years I have believed that our government and our Church have grown bankrupt. Now I work to responsibly withdraw my energy from systems already in decline and 'plant another row.'"

Initially, I had grave misgivings about *withdrawing* my energies in the face of injustice. It seemed to me that it was antithetical to *engaging* impasse. Then I came across the words of Albert Einstein. He said, "No problem can be solved from the same consciousness that created it."[33] Reflecting on his words brought me smack up against the limitations of both the leaders of our institutions and the institutional structures themselves. It shed light on words I have uttered all too often in the midst of the struggle: "They just don't get it." Of course, they don't! Our dominant societal institutions are driven by the radical miscomprehension that Earth is a collection of objects to be made submissive solely to the dreams and desires of the human. Thomas Berry, on the other hand, points to the deep "Livingness" *within* all creation when he says, "Earth is a *communion of subjects, not a collection of objects.*"[34] Finally it dawned upon me: Expecting existing institutions to engage in transformative systemic change while still enslaved in a consciousness that sees the other, both human and other-than human, solely as objects for our use is like asking the proverbial person who is blind to remove the plank from her/his *own* eye. It's not likely to happen. Over time I began to withdraw the energy formerly used to challenge dominant systems and focused it instead on creating alternatives grounded in an Earth-based consciousness. This thinking is no doubt related to some graffiti I saw scrawled across a building wall in New York City. It read, "Don't despair; just subvert." Creating alternative projects, programs, and even institutions seems to me to be a powerful way of *engaging* impasse and engendering enormous hope.

Rose Mary: What you say is quite interesting to me. Listening to you now and remembering the experiences of impasse that other participants shared brought me to an understanding of impasse as birthing creativity.

Margaret: That's fantastic! I love it. Can you explain it in more detail?

Rose Mary: For me engaging impasse is an invitation to analyze and name the mix of goods and evils, the beauty and the terror, in the situation faced. It is to awaken to the revelation of daily dawning. Such engagement calls me to touch into bodymindspirit to contemplate the interaction of the experience with me personally, with others, with Earth and with Cosmos. I try to ponder the situation within the larger universe story and intuit new possibilities for "ecojustice-ing." Engaging impasse as a tool of social analysis is like slowly turning a kaleidoscope and realizing the potential of interconnected possibilities. The disconnectedness, desolation, and terror of impasse gradually or sometimes spontaneously transform into connectedness, consolation, and hope.

> I began to imagine that there must be a precious vessel somewhere in this vast universe holding the tears, the suffering, and the love that these women and so many more have poured out on behalf of a better world....

Margaret: Yes, but not easily. There are very hard moments in engaging impasse. It can be *very* hard. I remember listening to the stories the women in our circle shared about their experiences of impasse. As I listened to story after story, three things happened to me.

First, I began to imagine that there must be a precious vessel somewhere in this vast universe holding the tears, the suffering, and the love that these women and so many more have poured out on behalf of a better world—much of it ultimately inspired not by some grand political schema but by the teachings of an obscure first-century carpenter from Nazareth. I felt a resolute conviction that none of it is in vain.

Second, I wanted to shout from the rooftops, "Women, thy name is Courage!" What many of these women might lack in upper body strength was surely overcome by the feminine creative and flexible counterpart to a steel-like tenacity to pursue justice for "these least of all," no matter what the personal cost.

Third, and most paradoxically of all, was the realization that at the very heart of the experience of impasse that each of these women shared was the reality that this very same and blessed desire for justice was so fraught with frustration—the frustration of not being able to achieve something inherently good. I left the first circle gathering with the vivid image of trying to crawl on hands and knees out of an angry, violent, and life-threatening surf, which unforgivingly throws you to the ground just as you appear to be gaining some footing. It was an image strangely reminiscent of my own personal experience of impasse.

Rose Mary: For me, Margaret, here is where contemplation comes in. Contemplation clears the cobwebs catching the prey of negative energy and discouragement that impasse can so often bring. It helps me to hold the positive energy and courage you spoke about which I agree was evident in the stories of impasse our group shared. It is contemplation that frees me to live with the questions, the paradoxes, the mysteries rather than

> Contemplation frees me to live with the questions, the paradoxes, the mysteries rather than focusing on the necessity of "solving impasse."

focusing on the necessity of "solving impasse." The gift of communal contemplation, which was so much a part of the program, really made me much more aware of the cosmic impact of positive energy as a power to engage impasse.

Margaret: I am really fascinated, Rose Mary, by your use of the phrase "the *cosmic* impact of positive energy." Ours is an era when the longer and larger *cosmic* story opens up whole new arenas for reflection, certainly regarding impasse, but also in other areas. This had a powerful impact on me when the war in Iraq juxtaposed itself between our first and second circle gatherings. Like others in our group, I was sickened by the political rhetoric leading to the war. For me this reaction was exacerbated by my participation in organizing and traveling to Iraq in 2000 as part of the U.S. Dominican Family's response to the decade-long sanctions against that country.

Shortly before the actual invasion, Nancy Sylvester, IHM wrote on our circle's electronic message board: "How are you holding [the possible war in Iraq] in a contemplative way? What are you learning when you engage this impasse in prayer?" I wrote in response,

> This morning I was reflecting on what happens when I place the imminent war in Iraq within the larger 13-billion-year universe story. In the very act of doing this, the realization opens that there is a larger universal wisdom and intelligence which when faced with crises more than once in the multi-billion year unfolding, transformed again and again. This

happened not without mass extinctions, and what appears from the perspective of puny human intelligence, to be an incredible waste of life. Yet we do know empirically that nothing is ever really lost in the compassionate embrace of the larger story.

This was no facile response on my part. I clung at this point by the skin of my teeth to the larger universe story and the much bigger God I had discovered through it.

As the war progressed and the second circle gathering approached, I remarked to several of my friends that were it not for the larger universe story, I felt I could lose my mind in the face of the barbaric spectacle that was unfolding in Iraq. To this very moment the above statement feels frighteningly real to me. While the universe story offered perspective in the face of impasse, it in no way lessened my grief, outrage, or public opposition to the war.

Rose Mary: And perspective is so important, isn't it? I am aware that, through the communal contemplation and dialogue during our gatherings and in the months afterward, it was pondering the new cosmology, the 13-billion-year-old unfolding of the universe and our role as humans in that unfolding, which nourished my spirituality and deepened my understanding of the relativity of the impasse. Incorporating cosmic consciousness rather than a limited linear timeline into my consciousness catapults ecojustice weaving from less of a deadend impasse into more of an unfolding challenge and opportunity. This is what I hear in the way you relate your experience regarding the Iraq war. The new cosmology enables us to let go of the enculturated, learned "otherness," and to experience primordial connectedness.

Margaret: Yes, and the paradox—and by the way, I believe engaging impasse is very much about living with equanimity in the space of paradox—is that the new cosmology creates a larger container for our experience of life and God, increasing our experience of connectedness in a way that can both intensify our grief, on the one hand, and "birth creativity," as you say, on the other. I find, though, that I

> I believe engaging impasse is very much about living with equanimity in the space of paradox....

must make a conscious effort to keep living and thinking in this broader context, especially with regard to engaging impasse. I wonder, Rose Mary, if you have that same experience?

Rose Mary: Yes, I do. I find that simple things help in this regard. Since perceiving connectedness is so much a part of the way I engage impasse in the context of the new cosmology, I often spend time contemplating connections in my personal experience. For example, the animals in Ecuador provide the wool in my sweaters; the pottery I treasure comes from many colors of soil and is made by our Native American sisters; laborers from around the world provide the food I eat. I often engage in an Earth-contemplation before meals and feel kin with soil and seeds; sprouts; leaves and stalks; farmers; raindrops and rainbows; sun, moon, and star light; clouds and wind; migrant workers and their families.

Walking the cosmic journey and sometimes facilitating it for others helps me to integrate bodymindspirit and enjoy my cosmic connections. Labyrinth walking connects me with ancestors, and also assists me with bodymindspirit integration and cosmic connecting. I find that labyrinthine letting-go, contemplation, insight, and commitment are metaphors for life as we experience it today. All of this strengthens my intuition that the personal and planetary are interconnected as closely as bodymindspirit. Barbara Marx Hubbard's words also motivate me: "We are coded not only with the memory of our personal prenatal history but also with our cosmic history."[35] This feeds me as I contemplate the profound implication of cosmic connectedness in relation to impasse and ecojustice-ing.

Cosmic connectedness also influences my choices of ministries. For more than a quarter century, I've been participating in systems transformation to help co-create a more just and equitable environment for all Earth's inhabitants. From hematite to halibut to humans, we share together Earth. How to be together, respecting our interconnectedness, requires engaging in systems analysis. Such participation is for me engaging impasse.

> Perceiving this cosmic connectedness is a key motivator for me in engaging impasse.

Perceiving this cosmic connectedness, Margaret, is a key motivator for me in engaging impasse. I sense something equally powerful for you in what you describe as "living with equanimity in the space of paradox." Would you say more about that?

Margaret: We both spoke about how the perspective of the new cosmology opens up a much larger container and thus relativizes things. Here is where impasse again powerfully connects with the new cosmology for me. If I learned anything from our circle gatherings, it is that impasse is an experience of extreme powerlessness that marks out the limits of being human in ways that are clearly a blow to what we formerly perceived. The new cosmology confirms this. Through it we learn that we humans are simply one aspect of the evolution of the life of the planet. Taken together these statements leave us with no surprise at the fact that *we* do not, indeed we *cannot* "solve" impasse. In our group, this led to voicing the conviction that "resolution" of impasse is truly the realm of the Divine.

Here comes the "other side" of the paradox. I recall vividly how breathtaking it was for us as a group to articulate that the above happens through none other than each of us! We laughed and squirmed as we said, "Yes, Ruthmary, Catherine, Patty…. (Yes, Reader), you are God." In an effort to ease our discomfort and embrace the truth of that statement we even quoted St. Catherine of Genoa who said, "My name is God."[36]

To say that we humans are simply one aspect of the evolution of the life of the planet has a corollary: We are at the same time those beings in whom Earth reflects on itself and in whose hands the future of life rests. Here is how Thomas Berry, speaking directly out of the new cosmology describes this understanding: "The Earth does not need us to produce a blade of grass, but we have reached a point where we will not have a blade of grass unless the human cooperates and conspires in its existence."[37]

All of this came together for me at a retreat I made a couple of months after our final circle gathering. A series of circumstances made it possible for me to visit Redondo Retreat Center located in the Jemez Mountains of New Mexico. One afternoon I visited what the locals call "The Tunnels." As I walked, to both my right and left, huge slabs of stone soared seemingly endlessly into the air. I felt very small but somehow that felt very right. Flying back to Long Island, days later, I scribbled on a napkin:

Departure morning after precious days of retreat.
Early "sit" gazing at The Mountain Teachers still
shrouded in darkness.
For days it was they who instructed;
some tree covered; others barren and stark; red ones too—
towering sages all, and swollen, as breasts filled by milk,
with the wisdom of the ages.

Teachers like none other are these; no lectures;
nonetheless eager are they to nurture.
Frolicking with light and sound and permanence,
they shatter the puny human mind
prying open eyes to hear and ears to see.
Enfolding the learner within the embrace of their being
one sucks of a wisdom The Mountain Teachers deign for
just this seeker.
his morning, though, there is of yet no light.

As if silenced by this on the day of leave-taking,
The Mountain Teachers
commission another:
White rays pierce the horizon, creeping over mountain
crests...
A waning crescent of the Wolf Moon rises.
A seal is placed upon all The Mountain Teachers taught.

The "wisdom deigned for just this seeker" so graciously imparted by The Mountain Teachers seems to me to be that engaging impasse is all about holding in the very same breath the awareness that we are, on the one hand, simply one aspect of the evolution of the life of the planet, and, on the other, that being in whom Earth reflects on itself and in whose hands the future of life rests.

Engaging impasse is about caring deeply, and in the same breath not caring. It is about working in a way that is focused on root causes of problems and having desired outcomes, and in the same breath, it is about letting go of all the outcomes. It is about allowing myself to be haunted by the unnecessary suffering of *all* life on the planet, yet it also is about acknowledging that suffering is part of the story. It is about resisting evil with all of my energy yet, in the same breath, it is about ultimately surrendering evil to the mystery of God. It is about resting in the long 13-billion-year story—and trusting the Divine that is at the heart of the story.

Rose Mary: Margaret, you just summarized for me what engaging impasse is in the context of the universe story: "Be-ing in the Story, trusting the Divine."

Rose Mary Meyer, BVM is an ecofeminist activist nourished by the universe story and the everywhere presence of the Divine. She currently coordinates Project IRENE, a nonviolence initiative of LCWR, Region 8.

Margaret Galiardi, OP is an Amityville Dominican who has focused her practice of theology on nonviolent initiatives for establishing right relationships among humans, and between humans and the natural world. She is currently staff person for Ecological Concerns at Siena Spirituality Center in Water Mill, New York.

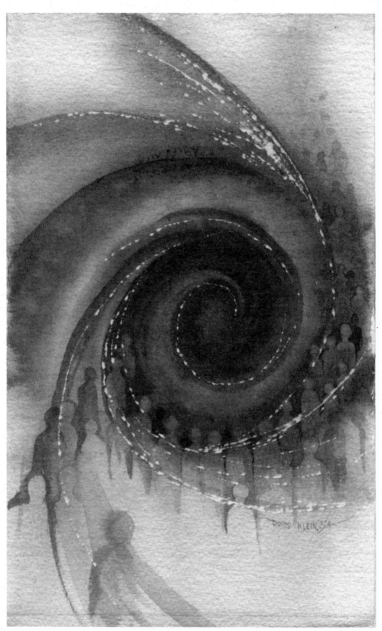

New Space Opened

Embracing Impasse and Her Sisters
Mary Hunt, Ph.D.

Nancy Sylvester's welcome invitations to join the first set of *Engaging Impasse* circles found my partner, Diann Neu, and me having to decide which one of us would attend. We both wanted to go, but with a newly adopted baby, and limited time and energy, we decided that only one of us could commit to it. Diann jokingly said, "You are so lacking in religious formation, *you* should go." I laughingly agreed, noting that it would not hurt my activist self to slow down and resume contemplative practice. I had enjoyed a meditation retreat at Rancho Vallecitos in New Mexico two years before. Yoga and meditation were part of my repertoire. Yet how quickly I had gotten out of the habit, with the pressing demands of work, family, and friends.

I found engaging impasse a necessary luxury for which I am deeply grateful. I was a member of one of the societal circles, a wonderful group of a dozen women from all over the country whose commitment to social change was matched by their rich spirituality. I considered myself an amateur at prayer in the company of these women, some of whom had spent decades in religious communities where spiritual practices are common. These women, now *compañeras* at a

97

distance, are a major reason why I came to embrace, not simply engage, impasse.

At the first meeting I entitled my story of impasse, "So Much More," to signal my frustration with the current social and ecclesial situations: war, pedophilia, and episcopal cover-up. I focused on the religious service held at the National Cathedral in Washington, D.C., shortly after September 11, 2001, where President George W. Bush all but declared war from the pulpit. The music, rhetoric, and readings at the service had a bellicose ring to them. Women religious leaders were absent save the accidental hostess, the interim bishop of the Episcopal Diocese, Jane Holmes Dixon, who was referred to as "James" on National Public Radio.

Everything that I hold dear and work to achieve—equality for all, abundance of life on this precious planet, religions as sources of love and justice—was violated in that unholy hour. I felt as if my work for twenty years in feminist theology at the Women's Alliance for Theology, Ethics and Ritual (WATER) had been for naught. But the pain was not just for me. It had a more cosmic feel, as if the abundant resources of this world had been squandered and there was seemingly little I could do about it. While I wept for my own disappointment, I wept for this larger sense that life could be so much more for so many more. I was up against impasse.

My companions told different stories. Some told of impasses with friends or community members. Others detailed political instances where a murder or war pushed them to the edge of despair. The content did not matter. We all, finally, had a common name for our experiences. What we needed and found in the process was the courage, support, and tools to engage impasse.

We began to look impasse in its steely eyes and choose how to approach it. We realized we did not have to confront head-on every unjust system, every recalcitrant individual. We could pick and choose without fear of co-optation. We could engage in non-violent, life-affirming ways of coping, in the process of making change. In rare but real instances, we could do nothing but pray, and that, somehow, was enough. These simple insights fell on our group of confirmed activists like rain on dry land.

At the second gathering I came to appreciate that the group was crucial to the "engaging" dimension of the process. We engaged on many levels—from our shared silence to the community stretching in yoga, from our common meals to our companion walks, from our critical analysis to our art projects. Music, prayer, symbols (like the powerful "She Who Watches" bowl) and our faithful return to the circle, session after session, rested or tired, knit us together. Any sense that contemplation was a privatized, individualized, apolitical approach quickly dissipated as substantive discussion ensued.

While I loved each member of my group, I came to value the collective as a kind of random community. Admittedly there was a certain self-selection in its composition—those who were eager to enter the process as I was. Nonetheless, there also a serendipitous quality to it. We could have been another dozen women. What mattered was that we used the resources we each brought and together we became more than the sum of our parts.

As a feminist liberation theologian I brought a certain intellectual and analytic strength to the group. What I received was equally important: the musical ability of one member, the artistic touch of another, the poetic imagination of one sister, the ecological commitment of another, the spiritual wisdom, mission experience, and justice work of others. The gestalt was rich beyond imagining, brought into focus by skilled, sensitive facilitators. I had the sense that it was not just a talented group. Rather, the methodological commitment of valuing and making space for the variety of gifts created space so that our individual strengths could be put to use for the common good.

Taken with Prayer

Many participants found the new cosmology materials on the origin and unfolding of our universe helpful for contextualizing the circle approach. Others found the dialogue aspect of the process useful. I, however, particularly appreciated the creative ways the facilitators gathered and synthesized responses from the group. We could all own the result without focusing unduly on our particular contribution to it. But overall, I found myself most taken with the prayer.

By the third circle gathering, with the meaning of impasse now obvious and engagement in high gear, it was time to deepen insights gained in the first two, and during the intervening time. My attention centered on prayer and meditation, their importance for my own life, and their centrality to healthy communities. If Diann were correct, that I was hopelessly deficient in formation, then there would be no better time to begin my remedial campaign! I had teachers galore and plenty to learn.

Prayer is something of an occupational hazard for theologians. Of course, it is expected as part of the profession that we will have a nodding acquaintance with diverse forms of worship used by religious people throughout the ages. But such objective knowledge is no substitute for a life of prayer. In fact, it can get in the way.

I struggle to keep my contemplation free of the scrutiny and evaluation I bring to theological issues. It is not easy. In the Catholic tradition, prayer, including the Eucharist, is often a source of deep pain and division for feminists. Part of my work is to understand and transform that dynamic so that women can be agents of our own religious lives. I have long had a heightened sense of responsibility to make sense of worship in order to make it accessible to all. But such work has its personal cost.

I decided at the circles to pay that cost no longer. I would consciously and happily suspend judgment in order to participate fully in rituals, both during the weekends and in my women-church group. Otherwise, I run the risk of understanding cognitively more than I experience spiritually. For example, I love to walk the labyrinth, enter into the prototypical journey, linger in the center of centers, and emerge refreshed. But I have to force myself *not* to think about the theo-political implications of the labyrinth spiritually for women: how easily we can be bought off with something that seems other-worldly and therefore not offensive; how commercialized even ancient spiritual models can be in a consumer culture; how easily we can be distracted from the needs of the here and now.

I am getting better at letting go of the analytic piece so I can participate in worship and draw on it for critical reflection. Ironically, this approach only enhances my ability to do my work. It does not render me uncritical; it permits me to choose when and where to exercise that capacity. It helps me to avoid the mini-impasses that line the way, and it provides me with the spiritual reserves to do my work over a long period of time.

Meditation is tough discipline for those of us who could be considered spiritually challenged! In Buddhist practice there is talk of the "Monkey Mind," that tendency in meditation to flit from thought to emotion to another thought at great speed. Perhaps we all do it: making a mental grocery list or singing a catchy tune in our minds when we are supposed to be en route to nirvana. The line between meditation and fantasy is sometimes thin. We monkeys are clever! I always pity the persons on either side of me in meditation because some Buddhist practitioners say that when you are distracted in meditation it is often the monkey mind of the person next to you! Regardless, the practice is not as easy as it looks. Practice is the right word for it because I find over time that the monkey loses steam and the focus is easier to achieve.

I crave silence now. I want more time to attend to my breathing and let my conscious mind take a rest. I do it in the oddest places—on the Metro en route to a meeting, in the pool during my morning laps. With practice, the concerns of the moment melt into the energy of the universe. I also find that I vary my walks around the neighborhood in direct response to one of our guided meditations. That exercise invited us to walk down unexplored paths. Discovering so many new avenues in my consciousness has prompted me to explore the physical neighborhood for what its unknown parts might reveal. I have not been disappointed.

One of my favorite meditation times comes in the evening when I put my little daughter, Catherine Fei Min, to bed. After we read stories and sing, Min likes one of her moms to cuddle her while she falls asleep. I use the time to meditate, which I consider an act of love and prayer. Our breathing together lulls her to sleep with the assurance that she is not alone, and neither am I. When Min is older, I plan to explain this to her in the hope that she will glean something about my spirituality. I think about this in light of my mother's habit of praying the rosary. We just gave her space and did not think too much about what seemed a quaint custom. Now I realize the significance of what my mother was doing and I admire her spiritual wisdom.

APPLYING THE PRACTICE

I have begun to incorporate contemplation into my teaching and lecturing. At a conference, I presented three ethical themes at three consecutive breakfast sessions. Instead of simply launching into a linear presentation, then inviting discussion, and finishing up with some conclusions, I played classical music by women composers in the background as we gathered. I began by inviting participants to spend a few minutes in silence. It was a popular move at an early hour when coffee and easing into the day were more on people's minds than my ethical agenda. The ringing of the Zen bowl to begin and end our meditation reverberated throughout the cavernous room, lending a certain intimacy to our meeting, a certain sacredness to our subsequent conversation. Then we proceeded apace with my presentation and our discussion. At the end of each session we sat in silence together. The practice encased the workshop with the equivalent of sacred bookends.

Many people remarked afterwards that they liked the format and felt it "fit" the justice-seeking ethical agenda I promoted. Most of us in theology are accustomed to walling off our intellectual pursuits from our spiritual practices. We did not all agree on the issues at hand, but there was a civility and attention to the discussion that might not have been there otherwise.

At a recent panel presentation one of my fellow panelists attacked what I had to say, making gratuitous remarks about my scholarly approach in order to bolster her own story-telling mode. I did not respond, choosing quite consciously to let her remarks pass rather than escalate what was obviously an impasse in the making. Several people approached me afterwards to assure me how out-of-bounds she had been. We had each been asked to address the topic as we saw fit, no one approach trumping the others. Rather than feeling duty bound to point out the obvious on the panel, and perhaps in so doing turning the tables, my studied silence spoke volumes, as the feedback from colleagues confirmed.

Many professional situations require a more aggressive approach to arguing through differences. But I am learning to discern more carefully what they are so as to focus energy and attention where it counts most. In this case, my silence spoke for itself and we were able to move on to matters of substance. Nonetheless, I wonder if I could have headed this off by incorporating some form of silence at the outset. Meditation provides intellectual breathing space, leveling the playing field. I feel no need to internalize blame for her thoughtlessness, but I do want to help to create the conditions in which many can flourish. One way to do that is to round out my default approach with some quiet.

I have begun to imagine how theological education and theological discussion might benefit from intentional incorporation of some of the *Engaging Impasse* techniques. Given how resistant to change institutions can be, I start realistically by trying out a few new approaches in WATER programs where feminist commitments to holistic learning invite such innovation. In fact, our focus on theology, ethics, *and* ritual makes our ambiance similar to that of the circles. We attend to environment, hospitality, and content with the same happy results. How to make this happen at the American Academy of Religion or the Catholic Theological Society remains to be seen. The American Friends Service Committee is doing something similar by creating online discussion groups to reflect critically on same-sex marriage. Quakers have considerable experience to share on the value of silence, and Catholics, among others, can learn from them.

I think faculty in theological schools and graduate programs could benefit from engaging impasse as they struggle to rethink theology in light of growing religious pluralism, more pointed demands from groups that have been marginalized in the field, and the increasing emphasis on religions as significant social organizations in a steadily more globalized world. I have no illusions that the cardinals will begin their deliberations in Rome for a new pope with soft music playing in the background, their eyes closed, their minds consciously focused on their breathing. But such an approach might lead them out of the impasse they assent to by participating in an exclusivist conclave. At best they will get another pope. With help, they could move into the fresh air of theological discussion about alternative models of church for which such restricted voting for a single leader would be unnecessary, indeed unthinkable.

No matter what other theologians and Church leaders do, I now live with uncertainty with more confidence. After all, answers to questions of ultimate meaning and value, the heart of theology, are approximations at best with certainty a figment of the imagination. Hence, it seems to me that the goal is not to be right, to prevail, or otherwise win in theology, but to find ways that we can live peacefully with our differences. I received some hints and glimpse of this in the circle where the variety of "goods," that is, the many different approaches and perspectives, combined to outwit even the most intractable impasse. It was not that problems vanished, rather that new space opened up to see them in relief and relativize their power.

> It was not that problems vanished, rather that new space opened up to see them in relief and relativize their power.

I find this approach so refreshing and empowering in contrast to the customary lose-lose set-up, that I have come to embrace impasse, perhaps hug it to death! My challenge is to find a balance between the critical reflection and constructive reshaping that are theology's task, and the insights that emerge from communal contemplation. They need not be mutually exclusive; they can be complementary in the most positive sense of the term.

I embrace my sisters in the process. Over our "last supper" as a group we had a frank, free-ranging discussion about our lives and ourselves. I doubt we could have had it without the circle practice and without the mutual respect and trust that had grown among us. It was a model for how differences can be aired and taken seriously, for how people can be heard and understood. Following the meal, we repaired to the dance floor. Our engagement was now a solid embrace of both impasse and one another, and we danced and we danced.

Mary E. Hunt is a Catholic feminist liberation theologian. She is the co-director of the Women's Alliance for Theology, Ethics and Ritual (WATER) in Silver Spring, Maryland. Mary teaches and writes on theo-ethical issues, serves on several editorial boards, and is active in the women-church movement. She is the author of FIERCE TENDERNESS and editor of several books, including the forthcoming A GUIDE FOR WOMEN IN RELIGION: MAKING YOUR WAY FROM A TO Z.

Time To Evolve and Deepen

Communal Quest Makes the Difference
Pat Kozak, CSJ

I was privileged to have a "sneak preview" of the *Engaging Impasse* project. The original planning group met at the center where my congregation has its administrative offices, including my own. I had the pleasure of meeting socially with them, and later with the Design Team (which included two friends with whom I live) who gave substance, art, and life to the project.

So it was not surprising that when the invitation to participate arrived in the mail, I already wanted to be a part of the project. This, however, did not translate as "without hesitation." As I became aware of the other participants in my circle and throughout the project, my own latent insecurity rose and I began to grapple with uneasiness at the prospect of being in a group with such "heavy hitters" and well-known figures. This hesitation is important because the shift that took place in me, as early as the first gathering, was a significant indicator of the power at work in this company of women, perhaps better stated as "the power at work in our companioning."

In considering what happened to me in the course of the *Engaging Impasse* circles, I need to ask an important question: Did the personal development that took

109

place at this time in my life happen *because* of the circles, or would this change have found me anyhow? Was it possible to distill the circle experience from the rest of my life and say, "this is now true because of that"? Looking back in search of an entry point into the experience and into these questions, I'm brought to the image of a doorway.

FINDING THE MISSING PIECE

I could have grown personally and professionally without the circles. A year earlier, I had made a particularly powerful directed retreat, which enabled me to reorient my life in an awareness of God's presence and a renewed sense of personal strength available to me. I was committed to draw on the intimacy and wisdom that were so near. So the question was a real one for me: why choose this next doorway, when to my mind, a much more profound threshold had already been crossed?

With or without participation in the circles, I am confident my own contribution to leadership would have continued to deepen in quality over the years of my ministry, as did those of my leadership team members. We had each attended a number of workshops to learn skills helpful to leadership roles, and learned processes and behaviors that were valuable. We were sincere about a commitment

> So the question was a real one for me: why choose this next doorway, when to my mind, a much more profound threshold had already been crossed?

to the Gospel values and the particular mission and charism of the congregation.

It was the *communal* element of the circle gatherings that provided the missing piece. Without that piece, much indeed would have been lost; much would have remained unseen. My own readiness—a readiness to explore how my own experience of personal transformation might extend to the level of the communal—was key to crossing this doorway. The circles provided the vehicle, and the particulars of the approach used to engage impasse were central to the experience. The cumulative effect of our communal

> It was the *communal* element of the circle gatherings that provided the missing piece.

sharings served to carry us through stages of development faster than any one story or reflection might. The degree of frustration and discouragement we felt became exponential. We recognized that our individual efforts to resolve impasse and conflict were not working and that we needed to approach impasse differently.

ENTERING A PLACE OF VULNERABILITY

Risks, even small ones, have their consequences. The women who gathered in my circle crossed over to a place of vulnerability and self-disclosure. We did so first by sharing personal stories of impasse, stories in which power was held unevenly and exercised unfairly. The anger, hurt, and outrage that surfaced as we recounted our stories of impasse, arose from a disregard or disrespect we had each experienced earlier, now captured in our stories. This disrespect seemed to reach far back, spanning a period longer than any one of us had lived, until it felt as though we were touching ancient hurt and loss.

As we remembered each of our stories, the disclosure took on the nature of a collective memory, a collective identity. The experiences of impasse, while occurring in particular time and space, took on a mythic dimension. Even as we experienced surprise and outrage at one another's stories of impasse in the Church, we recognized that we had each been there many times. The similarities of the stories, spanning thirty years, were compelling. Though a Vatican office gave way to a homey motherhouse meeting room, the boundary of a massive oak desk was replaced by a circle of living room furniture, and episcopal strangers became hometown clerics, the pattern of uneven relationships resulting in impasse was a constant. Time after time, despite committed efforts to the contrary, the conversations continued to be one-sided, the voice scolding, the attitude condescending. In one story, illustrative of all, a woman related how even a circle of chairs was rearranged to establish a clerical center. Our common ecclesial experience was of feeling invisible, insignificant, and powerless. Listening to each other's stories, we could close our eyes and be transported to and fro through thirty years of pain, claiming it as our own.

> The process was not magical or gimmickry. We listened intently—to words and to silence. We sat with each other in contemplative quiet.

The process was not magical or gimmickry. We engaged in dialogue. We listened intently—to words and to silence. We sat with each other in contemplative quiet. We watched and waited and tested our insights and vision. Competition was non-existent, perhaps because achievement was not a goal. We developed, without conscious intention, a deep regard, respect, and genuine affection for each other. At the same time, it did not become a social network; I see only one of the fourteen women in my circle with any frequency in a professional setting. However, at each gathering of the circle, the bonds that connected us in our previous meeting had deepened and we experienced that our delight at coming together again was real and tangible. Overall, I experienced a process and insights that were transferable. But they were not, in themselves, solutions to impasse nor were they experiences of personal transformation in and of themselves.

LOOKING DIFFERENTLY

The circles process *was* a doorway, and as such had the potential to lead to another side, to open to another perspective, another reality. And that is what happened for me and for the other women in my circle.

What I have noticed that I can attribute in some significant way to the experience is that, first and simply, I look around, I see, *more slowly*. Contemplation is sometimes referred to as taking "a long, loving look at the real." I find that I am looking more slowly, with greater attention, whether it is at people or situations,

processes, or questions. I am not expecting or requiring the answer to appear immediately after the question. In fact, over the course of the year in which we
met, I increasingly began to notice an evolution of an
awareness or consciousness in me in response to questions, and then, more slowly, the surfacing of an
answer that might prove helpful.

The value of allowing time for consciousness to
evolve and deepen may seem obvious, but for someone whose mind automatically moves to solutions and
responses as soon as a need surfaces, this added reflec-
tivity was decidedly different. To stay with the question or experience and allow multiple responses and
perspectives to come forward—this was different. To
gradually allow something, maybe a whole new
notion, to surface above the rest, rather than intentionally shape it from the onset—this was different. I also
began to notice that the minor upsets around me often
elicited calm and reassurance rather than matching
upset. These responses and behaviors were not universal or across the board; nor were they always apparent
to those around me, although some change was
noticed. I was more aware of slowing down from
within; looking more slowly; looking longer; allowing
some natural rhythm to emerge through the events of
the day, rather than imposing one.

Praying Differently

The style of my prayer shifted. It was increasingly
a keeping-company—with God, with the holy, with
my own breathing as linked to the Breath of God
within me, and with all the issues and concerns and

114

people in my life. Prayer gradually became more intimate even as it became larger—encompassing wider needs, a sense of the whole and the universal, while never losing a sense of a profound intimacy with a personal God. It was as if the space or being of my person was larger than life and that this being was situated in a still larger reality that was strangely intimate and personal in its depth.

While Scripture continued to be a frequent starting place for prayer, there was more quiet, as the words of Scripture would drop away. Sometimes the appeal of Scripture would be replaced by an attraction to the images of poetry, *e.g.*, the poetry of Mary Oliver, John of the Cross, Hafiz, and David Whyte.

A simple refrain, like the following from John of the Cross, sometimes served as a mantra-like invitation to a quiet presence that was both restful and powerful.

> *How gently and lovingly*
> *you wake in my heart,*
> *where in secret you dwell alone,*
> *And in your sweet breathing, filled with good and glory,*
> *how tenderly you swell my heart with love.*[38]

Prayer was occasionally the invitation to welcome into my company persons or issues that were troublesome or painful. Sometimes these were real people on the national or international stage whose presence in my prayer was a way of inviting in the major issues of conflict and impasse of the day. During the Iraq war, I found myself "inviting" President Bush and Saddam Hussein into the place of my prayer to share the same place and time, and in some way, breathe in each other's company. I believed that if I could draw on the presence and breath of God while in the presence of these two men who represented for me such conflict and impasse, then perhaps some healing could happen in me, in them, in the world affected by them, simply by sharing the peace, power, and breath of God's presence.

Other times, I was led to invite my everyday companions or colleagues into the place and time of prayer. While not possessing the notoriety of world leaders, together, we were sometimes characters caught in conflict, struggle, and impasse. To be able to invite them into this space and not work the conflict, but simply allow or acknowledge their presence, was healing and strengthening. In some mysterious way, what often resulted was a rediscovery of a simple and genuine love for these individuals, a love that was of the heart rather than the head.

I found myself rising earlier in the morning and experienced increased energy over this span of time. I believe this energy shift is related to the increased time given over to quiet prayer and to the practice of "looking more slowly" at the issues and realities around me.

LEADING DIFFERENTLY

In retrospect, I also can see specific impact on my ministry in congregational leadership. I found myself shaping committee meetings to include a significant amount of time at the beginning for members to tell "stories" or share experiences that might bring us into a shared space before we actually began the "work" of the committee. This coming into a common space seemed to enhance the ease and trust in the group, which in turn enabled concerns and questions to be explored without judgment and in ways that were enriching and creative.

The group was comfortable exploring broadly the issues at hand, without needing immediate outcome or closure. Later, when closure was needed, the "answer" most suited to the common good often became apparent: Decisions surfaced around the "rightness" of the shape and substance of financial support for a sponsored ministry, the process most appropriate for election of congregational leaders, and the necessary next step in a still unfolding plan for a new ministry.

While few, if any, of my committees or groups formally used a dialogue process, I sometimes found myself actively encouraging a common search for the question or concern that might underlie the struggle or issue, and to do so with a genuine curiosity and desire for wisdom and enlightenment.

Knowing What You Have To Do

In the fable, *The Illustrated Alchemist*, by Paulo Coelho, the main character comes to believe that "when you want something, all the universe conspires in helping you to achieve it." The young man also learns that to "realize one's Personal Legend is a person's only real obligation. All things are one."[39] Attentiveness and the openness to recognize the elements as they present themselves are essential. It is an attitude of watching, waiting, and entering into life—without coercion or constraint—that enables wisdom. What is required is the discipline and courage to listen with one's whole being, not just with intellectual acuity. This discipline and courage is essential to knowing when it is time to speak and to act.

Participating in the circle gatherings was not simply an exercise of personal and professional growth; it was an experience of entering into a deepened faith in the Spirit of God, active in each of us as circle members. It was a personal choice and relational commitment.

The experience of intimacy and solidarity had begun with "a long, loving look at the real." It moved us, individually and collectively, to a commitment "to speak the truth in love" despite multiple voices within and outside, urging compromise, appeasement, or confrontation.

I know I am standing differently, moving differently, looking differently. I find that I engage in fewer debates and less argument. I feel myself standing "in my own place" with a calm that is new for me. This sense of self and its accompanying calm are true whether it involves straightforward communication with a bishop or with members of my congregation. While this choice to "speak the truth in love" often brings with it a certain clarity of thought, I am also aware of feelings in myself of affection for the other, and personal confidence. Absent are attitudes of confrontation or challenge.

I realize how many good people are near at hand; how many of these people are trying very hard to change the world or change themselves—or both. This recognition of companionship and solidarity contributes to an energy, an almost visceral sense of power and tangible hope, that we, as individuals, as a circle, as a people, are on the verge of an in-breaking. It is an in-breaking that paradoxically feels as if it were taking place from the inside out. I am aware that my vision has changed, as if new lenses had replaced the old, and the vision evokes its own power and confidence.

BEING PRESENT AT THE BORDERS OF COLLAPSING SYSTEMS

Where this continuing experience will take me is uncertain. However I believe, along with social commentators, futurists, and mystic poets, that the systems and institutions of which we are a part are terminally ill. Weighed down by harmful structures and world views that inhibit healing and creativity, these social, ecclesial, and political structures are not likely to throw off that which makes them ill in order to become healthy. Dying, however slowly, they often manifest desperation and efforts at frantic control. They are, all the same, terminally ill.

> I believe it is essential to stand at the borders of these collapsing and dying systems and simply be present there, without confrontation or animosity or fear. I believe our presence there will provide a place of meeting and discovery.

In their place, new communities and new structures will be needed, founded on values of mutual respect, shared wisdom, a commitment to justice, and a hope implicit in the Gospel and the power of God's Spirit.

I believe it is essential to stand at the borders of these collapsing and dying systems and simply be present there, without confrontation or animosity or fear. I believe our presence there will provide a place of meeting and discovery. It will be a gathering place for those who want to be faithful to that which is being revealed in a shared, long, loving look at the real. These gathering communities will be circles of welcome and grieving, as both the dying and rising happen side by side. Finally, these gatherings will be communities of hope, living into a vision not yet fully seen.

A native of Cleveland, Ohio, Pat Kozak, CSJ, D.Min., entered the Congregation of Sisters of St. Joseph of Cleveland in 1964, and is currently serving a second term as a member of its Leadership Team. She has taught high school theology and served in vocation and formation ministries. While studying in Berkeley, California, Pat spent eleven "wonderful years" in the

 East Bay area, working as part-time pastoral associate and spiritual director, offering group facilitation with accompanying prayer and ritual for a variety of religious and Church groups. When not engaging in one of these activities, Pat enjoys conversation with friends, poetry, gardening, and an occasional home repair project.

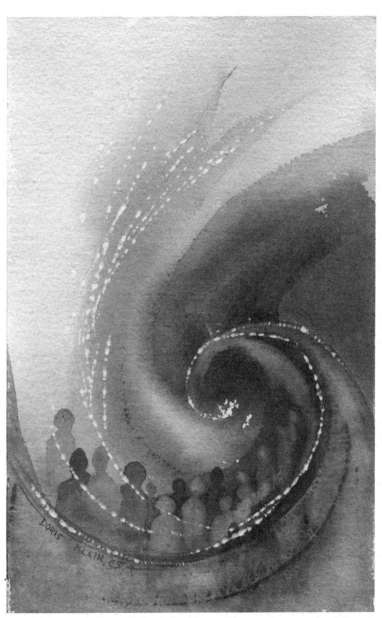

New Naming, New Energy, New Hope

A New Energy, A New Hope

Elinor Shea, OSU

"Why do you want to be part of a circle?" the response form asked. My heart opened and my responses poured out:

> My own experience of impasse, my conviction of the isolating impact of living in the impasse without a contemplative community, my hope that my work done in spirituality, justice, and spiritual direction training over the past twenty years will be confirmed, deepened, and expanded, my desire to be faithful to the call this invitation represents, my passage through impasse in AA recovery, my fear of the grip of despair, my love for the Church—all these draw me powerfully to seek participation.

Why such an outpouring? What was behind it?

With my first reading of Connie FitzGerald's article, "Impasse and Dark Night,"[40] in 1984, a place had been touched in me, deeper than my own awareness, a neuralgic spot, inaccessible and unnamable to me at the time. The invitation to be part of a circle for engaging impasse resonated in that same place. In 1984, I was writing an article on spiritual direction and social consciousness,[41] a narrative describing the vision, development, and practice of forming spiritual directors at the Center for Spirituality and Justice, located in the Bronx, New York. The particular genius of this program was to develop a wider lens for spiritual directors to use in contemplating the experience of their directees, moving beyond the usual intrapsychic and interpersonal range to include experiences in the societal and public arenas. The intent was to find a linkage between spirituality and justice in those seeking direction, and to develop this approach in potential directors. So the societal and ecclesial dimension of impasse, dark night, and transformation as described by FitzGerald, seemed to support and greatly enhance our emerging vision.

But what of my own experience of impasse? As I reflect on the intervening years, from 1984 to 2002, I am now able to see that while my attention and social analysis skills were consistently drawn to the importance of societal structures, my energies in ministry were spent in the work of spiritual direction, which appeared to be so "private." My article expressed rather clearly the significance of the transformation of structures, the inclusion of work for justice as an integral expression of faith. But despite this clarity, or perhaps because of it, I found myself experiencing a kind of dissonance between that conviction, which I continually tried to explore and act within, and my own specific ministry. I felt it as a deep 'dis-ease,' which no amount of analysis, spiritual direction, or working toward recovery through Alcoholics Anonymous (AA) could dislodge or dispel. There was a deeply internalized judgment of failure at the critical place of self-understanding and acceptance—thus my personal impasse. I entered the process with these feelings of ambivalence, as well as with a deep longing and a small grain of hope.

EXPERIENCING IMPASSE BEFORE I KNEW ITS NAME

At the initial gathering of our circle, we were invited into smaller subgroups where we told the story of our own personal impasse. In my story, I recounted an event that took place in 1967, in Rome, thirty-six years earlier. So long ago, and yet I knew I had no choice but to tell it, once again. It had been revisited so often and so fruitlessly. I described a choice I had made in response to conditions imposed by the leadership team in my province for my acceptance and ongoing membership in my congregation, this sixteen years after my initial embrace of our life.

I had come to Rome from a world of active involvement in Vietnam war protest, civil rights organizing, engagement with the poor and the war on poverty—the world of Vatican II, a world of expanding horizons and visions and hopes for transformation of structures. I was there for a tertian year, a final year of formation and a preparation for pronouncing solemn vows. My hope and intention upon returning to my province was to open a center in the South Bronx that would serve as link between the inner city and our college (the College of New Rochelle), and provide a ground for developing social consciousness and action for our students and ourselves. The condition imposed by the leadership team—that I work within the limits of our apostolic work at that time, in education, and, specifically, in our schools—meant an abandonment of this dream. For the sake of acceptance, approval, and membership in the congregation—a vocation I also believed was mine—I accepted. It was an experience of impasse before I knew its name. From that point until I engaged the impasse through the circle gatherings, I was held in a place of conflict, a place I had been brought to by an act of apparent surrender, which insistently felt like an act of submission and cowardice.

In the storytelling process, my story was received without judgment, advice, reframing, dismay, or a million other repressive possibilities. The intensity of feelings, of pain and anguish, that each woman's story held was taken into this circle of contemplation, aided by the wisdom and loving kindness of the Tonglen,[42] a Tibetan practice given to assist the process of cultivating an all-embracing heart of compassion. In a way that first appears counter-intuitive, Tonglen links the flow of breath directly to suffering—one's own and that of all beings—as a way of opening to the fullness of the suffering and of offering relief and care. The process afforded us a way of hearing and receiving one another's story of

> My story was received without judgment, advice, reframing, dismay, or a million other repressive possibilities.

impasse without being totally overcome or becoming defended in the face of so much pain. The processes prepared for the rest of that first gathering—silent communal contemplation, conversation, yoga, and facilitated dialogue—held each of us and each story in a safe and steady circle of shared pain where we could develop trust, and where quiet amazement grew, amazement that each life could sustain so much and yet go on, far beyond mere survival. We had touched "the grief that never leaves you," described in the invitation to *Engaging Impasse*. We were willing to go on together, supported by these alternating modes of presence, as well as those informal moments of laughter and spontaneous interactions, which increased our ease with one another and with the process.

> Insights born of contemplation do not necessarily come at the moment one is engaged in the practice; they may come at unexpected times and places.

The project had an excellent website (www.engagingimpasse.org), filled with a wide range of resources and a specific conversation board accessible to participants in each circle. Contrary to my expectations, I did not access the website to any significant degree in the time between the sessions nor did I, or any of the other members of my circle, use the conversation board. The level of participation and communication at the second and third sessions, however, made it clear that we actually were engaged in a profound way at an unconscious level where the energies of transformation were at work. At each successive meeting, our presence to one another, our communication, our contemplative prayer and dialogue testified to the hidden work being done in us while we continued to meet the challenges of our daily lives and ministries.

This remains a very significant teaching for me about expectations, and about the dark abyss where faith works. Insights born of contemplation do not necessarily come at the moment one is engaged in the practice; they may come at unexpected times and places.

DESCENDING TO PLACES OF TRUTH

The actual experience of the second gathering of our circle is less detailed and nuanced in my memory. Since most of the women in my circle were actively engaged in congregational leadership, they brought experiences of struggle with the hierarchical ecclesial structures, both external and internal. There was a ready empathy for one another's stories, a shared sense of courage in the face of all the evidence of oppression, exclusion, and dismissal. The sexual abuse scandal had highlighted so dramatically the compromised leadership of the American bishops.

Sitting together once more in the circle of communal contemplation, I experienced our descent into prayer, as our chant described it, "falling into the darkness of impasse...waiting in the darkness of impasse, letting God's silence seep...awaiting our God within..."[43] The descent was rapid, so it seemed to me, to a place familiar though daunting. This prayer and the subsequent processes planned by the Design Team were well suited to enable us to explore the darkness together and acknowledge our own complicity in the impasse. A combination of structured dialogue, listening to one another, mapping the terrain, walking silently in meditation in prepared spaces, holding places like the labyrinth, and returning to our silent communal contemplation supported us in the descent to the places of truth.

Key for me was an exercise in which we were asked to get in touch with the emotions we feel in the experience of impasse, and why we feel so, with the instructional invitation to "go to the places that scare you."[44] Identifying my emotion regarding impasse and repeatedly asking why I felt this way, led me to a place of radical emptiness—a place that terrified me, that I had persistently resisted, and that, paradoxically, I discovered myself already to be in. I left that session rooted in this place of radical emptiness, recognizing for the first time that it was a place I was incapable of inhabiting without negative judgment. Coming into this awareness was a huge relief. I wrote, "I don't feel I can go to that place. Rather I have discovered or am discovering that I am already there, and when that happens and I recognize it, I feel relieved of a great burden." Perhaps this could become a place of rest and acceptance, rather than the familiar terrain of harsh judgment, failure, and defeat.

Since then, Denise Levertov's poem, "Primary Wonder," has come into my life, meeting me in that place of emptiness and somehow stabilizing my willingness to stay there and go on in the process.

> *Days pass when I forget the mystery.*
> *Problems insoluble and problems offering*
> *their own ignored solutions*
> *jostle for my attention, they crowd its antechamber*
> *along with a host of diversions, my courtiers, wearing*
> *their colored clothes; cap and bells*
>
> > *And then*

once more the quiet mystery
is present to me, the throng's clamor
recedes: the mystery
that there is anything, anything at all,
let alone cosmos, joy memory, everything
rather than void and that, O Lord,
Creator, Hallowed One, You still,
hour by hour sustain it. 45

The presence of "the quiet mystery," experienced in our circle of communal contemplation, reveals and reassures that we are all sustained "hour by hour" by the Creator.

At the close of the second gathering, we gave expression to our pain in a ritual of lament, anguish, protest, cries from the abyss of darkness, and crushing powerlessness—a prayer for exorcism. The way was opening in the darkness, not seen so much as felt. I left the gathering drained, empty, confused, but also somehow hopeful, profoundly grateful for the strength and wisdom of the holding process. I was truly engaged in impasse.

During the time between the second and third sessions, I was kept in this place of emptiness, and was revisited by all my old demons of negativity, self-centered fear, paralysis, and despair—"my courtiers, wearing their colored clothes; caps and bells ... jostle for my attention." In my daily living, I was surrounded by women who were passionately involved in faithful prayer and action, protesting the war, the rape of the environment, the abuse and neglect of women and children. I felt useless, immobilized, envious, ashamed, weak. I was in that place that scared me and I could not escape. These familiar undermining adversaries were there, too, attacking my ministry of spiritual direction as irrelevant, misguided, a betrayal of my "real" call; pulling and seducing me into old feelings of uselessness, envy, self-generated ambition. Writing about it even now stirs some of that fear, terror, dread. There was no escape; this force is stronger than I. My "house" had been swept clean (Luke 11:24-26), or so it seemed to me, by the process of our second gathering and ritual.

Fortunately, the graced structure of AA continued to provide me with a strong container, a place were I could bring my experience, a place where powerlessness is the price of admission. I was also sustained in a truly powerful way by the persistent and unconditional love of friends, two in particular, who opened to me their experience of love and grief, "that grief that never leaves us." Being together in a loving embrace allowed us to endure our particular griefs and steadied us to go on along the path of darkness. These conversations and the forecasting energy of ongoing dreams made this time bearable and gave me the capacity to let the purifying work go on.

> The way was opening in the darkness, not seen so much as felt.

IMPASSE RADICALLY TRANSFORMED

As I approached the third circle gathering, I found that out of the prayer of those intervening months, I had come to an acceptance of a familiar yet strangely new self-awareness, identity. Expressed for me in the language of the First Week of the Spiritual Exercises of St. Ignatius, I knew myself, felt myself, accepted myself, and felt accepted by God as a loved sinner— no longer an imposter, a fraud. From that place and identity, I was able to embrace as my own, the words my recently widowed friend had spoken to me about her new experience of herself: "I'm no longer going to describe myself as who I used to be." A new naming, a new energy, a new hope.

There was a joy and relief for me in coming together again in our circle. I believed that we had all been affected by our engagement in this process, without our understanding how. The container so skillfully prepared for us by the Design Team would make it possible for us to discover how "the Mystery we call God," to use Karl's Rahner's[46] expression, had been at work in us. The words of our chant, "Falling into the darkness of impasse, we enter silence deep.... There we await our God within, birthing the new..."[47] ushered us into the place where discovery could happen, where we could access new energy, new vision. The words of St. John of the Cross, which marked the opening of the session, described the texture of our presence to one another: "Contemplation is nothing other than a secret, peaceful, loving inflow of God. If given room, it will fire the soul in the spirit of love."[48]

Perhaps because the Design Team had shaped our process out of their own experience, they were emboldened to ask us what had been shifting in our experience of impasse during the intervening months, what was dawning on us, what skills we were being taught for living in impasse. Their question was "what" not "whether," and their encouragement facilitated our being able to name our experience. Some of this was expressed in broad strokes which left much room for interpretation, observations such as:

> I am remembering what I didn't know I knew...I am drawn to surrender to the call to be vulnerable rather than empowering the impasse by struggling with it...anger against is becoming anger for...there is a shift going on, not a shift in a strategy but a movement of perception and consciousness...a lighter touch and increased intensity...we need a new body, a new incarnation and a new Eucharist...surrendering what gets in the way of contemplation, communal contemplation....

Along with these we gathered invaluable insights, tools, and practices to keep our new terrain free from old habits of un-freedom. Collectively, we were gathering strength and energy—invaluable, practical, poetic, functional tools—for the rest of our journeys. On a very personal note, one of my circle companions offered me an intuitive recasting of my new name from "loved sinner" to "sinful lover." Remarkable how that reversal of adjective and noun liberated a joy in me that endures. This recasting also gave me a deeper and richer appreciation of my own appropriation of, "I am no longer going to describe myself as who I used to be."

We were invited to identify shifts in energies, activities, characteristics, symbols, metaphors, strength, resources, practices, and disciplines. A harvest poured out of us as we gathered the fruits of the process thus far. For me, the concluding hours were full—full of energy, laughter, tears, wisdom, rituals, and appreciations. There was a sense of completion of a process, which was so deeply interior that without knowing exactly how, my own experience of impasse has been radically transformed and I live in this awareness. When I try to express it, it comes out something like this: "On some level, nothing has changed, and on another level, everything!"

THE LIBERATING YOKE OF MY MINISTRY

And what of the days and months since? How has this experience affected the perspective I bring to my ministry of spiritual direction? In rereading my own article, "Spiritual Direction and Social Consciousness," I recognize and truly embrace with a radically different quality of freedom the grace and call of this ministry, which has been given to me. Perhaps I have at last, finally, surrendered my attachment to "a better version of myself," an attachment born of a false consciousness and ego-based identity, one that would have had me heroically leading the troops to the barricades of systemic injustice. Dramatic? Of course! Ego-reinforcing? To be sure! Fruitful and confirmed by God? No, not during all those years. All the while the true gift and call were continually offered to me, the gift of the liberating yoke of my ministry, placed there by God on my stiff, resistant, and stubborn shoulders. This is the attachment that had to be broken, but broken nonviolently through the process of communal contemplation and dialogue. It had yielded to nothing else. And so I bring to my ministry new joy and humble gratitude, returning to that place and knowing it for the first time.[49]

Nothing I had written about the work of spiritual direction before was untrue, only incomplete. The gift of simultaneity is widened now to embrace ecological consciousness, a fuller vision being revealed through the new cosmology, the 13.7-billion-year story of the unfolding of the universe and our role as humans in it. "The Mystery we call God" continues to be self-revealing and self-donating in and through our daily human experience. Our call, still so clearly expressed in the 1971 Bishops' Synod statement, "action on behalf of justice and participation in the transformation of the world fully appears to us as constitutive dimensions to the preaching of the Gospel,"[52] continues to inform and challenge our understanding of faith in action, our true praxis.

DELICIOUS IRONY AT WORK

I come to my work now much more aware of the field of energy in which we all live and move and breathe. I experience in my whole being a remarkable new energy for life. I believe I know better how to perceive impasse at work in those I serve as a director, seeing the impasse as part of the whole energy field, not its barrier. I have a different faith in the necessity of surrender in contemplative prayer, not because I really understand it but because I have experienced in a new way the power of being part of a circle of communal contemplation and dialogue. I can cherish and reaffirm my experience of it in my local community. I can much more freely be present to others as they engage in their ministries, especially those directly focused on transformation of societal and ecclesial structures. I genuinely rejoice in the great variety of gifts and talents, attractions and commitments, all on behalf of our wounded world and wounded Church.

There is also a delicious irony at work here. Now that I have been freed from the deadening power of the impasse, I am now, by my own offering, facilitating the process of long-range planning and change for my province. This is an offer I could not have made as recently as a few months ago. Whatever energy has been released in me has moved me to service in that capacity, along with my work of spiritual direction. The breakthrough in impasse for me has been a grace of liberation from a delusional grandiosity and the gracious gift of my life to be lived simply and wholeheartedly on life's terms.

Elinor Shea, OSU is a member of the Eastern Province of the Roman Union of Ursulines. She lives in the South Bronx in a small community. Elinor has worked for over twenty-five years as a spiritual director and trainer and supervisor of directors, with a particular emphasis on identifying and developing the essential connections between spirituality and justice and the spirituality of the Twelve Steps.

With a Cloud of Witnesses

The Horizon Just Before Dawn
Margaret Swedish

My heart is moved by all I cannot save:
so much has been destroyed... [51]

Adrienne Rich

I carry their stories, stories of the dead, the martyred—stories of the tortured and the disappeared, stories of their loved ones, the survivors of massacres, parents who lost their children, children who lost their parents, sisters who lost their brothers, colleagues whose friends were taken away and never seen again. I have carried them for twenty years in my work with the Religious Task Force on Central America in Washington, D.C.

So many dead, so much loss, so much suffering. I used to know what they were dying for—for the liberation of their people. I don't know anymore what it was for.

I have carried their stories, and people looked to me for hope, to find in the death and grief something salvific, something that gives meaning to this sacrifice.

I carry their stories and the stories of their people, those who believed in the dream—the dream of liberation—where the price paid in blood was supposed to produce the harvest of justice, the joy of poor people set free of oppression. "May my blood be a seed of liberty," proclaimed Archbishop Oscar Romero the month before his assassination in March 1980.[52]

But the hoped-for liberation did not occur—and won't, for a very long time, if ever. The dictators are gone for now, but the oppression, the injustice, the poverty, remain. Somewhere along the road of this solidarity journey, that realization crept up like a dark shadow, not only in me but in so many others, who also could not give themselves permission to let it rise to the surface, take a good look at it, and come to terms with what it means for us.

I do not carry their stories alone. I have never carried their stories alone. Stories are what made our movement, our struggle, so rich, so human, so passionate. Stories are what we carry in our hearts, what we share—an intimacy among us as among family, a close circle of friends. I have carried them in a community of solidarity, in friendships formed over years of shared work and struggle. We have walked through fear and grief and pain together, so many of us.

I carry these stories to impasse—as a people, as community, as friends and colleagues—I come to impasse still not alone. I come to impasse with a cloud of witnesses, a community in grief, a community perplexed that, for all that was done and all that was given, we could not change the world, even the relatively small world of Central America.

SHARING GRIEF, DESPAIR, DISILLUSIONMENT

I chose to accept the invitation to engage impasse because it came to me in the very place and moment of that perplexity and disillusionment, this sense that the evil we sought to overcome was far more powerful than our best efforts and their greatest sacrifices. I came to a circle of friends and colleagues to find a space to say this out loud—that I was in grief, that all we did failed to make the world better, that many of us had come to a place of hopelessness, of helplessness that was too terrible to look at from the vantage point of the martyrs, the massacred—too hard to say, okay, we step back from this in order to re-think what we are doing.

I entered a circle of shared grief, disillusionment, disappointment, cynicism, and despair. These are words I have dared not to say aloud because I feared that if I did I would bring them to life in others, and that's not what this community has looked to me to find. It has been my special burden, at times—that so many have looked to me for hope.

I have seldom been able to pronounce these words out loud—until coming to this safe space of communal contemplation engaged with others who have come to impasse. The grief and disillusionment, the experience of loss, that was spoken in our stories of impasse rose to the surface not only in me but in a circle of colleagues and friends who already knew this grief, recognized it immediately, and thus gave it more life, more vivid life, than I thought I could bear.

Here was my story, a memory seared into my soul, of Father Jim Carney taking me aside one night in June 1983 in Managua, Nicaragua, telling me that he would soon return to Honduras, the country from which he had been exiled, that he would return clandestinely to be part of a revolutionary movement to help liberate the Honduran people from military dictatorship, an utterly hopeless venture. I carried the burden of that knowledge, his secret shared with me in trust, the burden of knowing that it was foolhardy and that I would probably never see him again.

Three months later he was disappeared. We learned many years later that he was captured by soldiers, tortured, and probably thrown alive from a helicopter.

In that space of our circle, exactly twenty years later, the extent of the grief stunned me. I had shared this story before, surely, but had never come to terms with the emotions that had lain buried all these years. It was for Jim, and it was for all of them in him, all of them.

My story of disillusionment and grief met those of others in that circle, grief and this perplexity and wonderment that these structures and relationships of injustice were not changed, for all the best efforts of so many good people.

And so we wept. In the safe space of our circle, newly formed, we wept, and then went into silence and into prayer, while She Who Watches[53] held our grief tenderly, without judgment, so that we could open it in a space of trust, to see what it had to teach us. In community with others who know, it took on flesh, became inescapable and incarnated.

Communal contemplation created this "space." Alone, in contemplation, I sit with my impasse; I carry it as my unique burden, a loss of heart, an infidelity. Was it not a betrayal of "them," those whose stories I carry?

In the sharing of my story of Jim, this torrent of grief-never-fully-faced overwhelmed me. As it touched the grief and hopelessness and sense of waste that others in the circle felt, I realized it was not only *my* truth, *my* burden. It signaled a truth in others, a signature moment of impasse in the work of solidarity.

Once named, affirmed, embraced, it became all the more inescapable and vivid.

The bond created by this shared grief was extraordinary and set a dynamic that remained throughout our process together—an incredibly gentle and tender space of trust where we knew we had permission to say the things in our hearts. The pain that was shared awed us, we caressed it gently, and so was the trusting space of the circle created.

And in this mutual listening around these lost dreams and hopes, we could say those things we did not think we had permission to say. For social justice activists, human rights workers, solidarity workers, to say it did not work, that lives were given for no better future, that we did not change the world, is to find ourselves on our knees with this question of what it was all for.

For us, the fear of failure is rooted in the reality of the human costs of failure. It is hard, then, to give oneself permission to acknowledge impasse, much less engage it.

TIME FOR A PROFOUND LETTING-GO

What happened for me was that a loving, trusting space was created, where what was in my heart about all of this could finally surface, be articulated, and I could simply be in it, let it have its life, let it begin to find expression, let it carry me rather than thinking any longer that I could carry it.

I had been resisting this for some time, this need to pull back to the interior life, to a quiet space, to listen to all that happened, all that they/we did, and all that has meant/means for me. When the space was created, the honesty of these doubts and struggles came immediately to the surface, a deluge.

In our circle, in our contemplation, our silence, our dialogue, I found the reassurance that my burnout was not my singular failure or a sign of personal weakness. Instead, it was a "sign of the times." It spoke to something truly important occurring on this journey, and it was in this space of shared contemplation and extraordinary "listening" that it could begin to be explored in community.

For some of us, there is this awareness that we have entered a time when a profound letting-go is required—letting-go of a whole way of thinking about our world. This echoed in our circle. And some of it was harsh—because, in this work of solidarity, confronting powers of repression, brutality, dictatorship, and war, we learned a lot about what human beings are capable of doing to each other, how self-destructive we can be, how it seems that we do not have the spiritual strength or the basic survival instincts to pull ourselves back from the brink.

We have arrived at impasse through years of struggle and hard work. What happened for me in this tender circle was that, in going into the impasse rather than trying to avoid it, I found it not dead or empty but vivid and vibrant and terrible.

Engaging impasse seems to contradict the very thing that the activist is trying to do—to effect change. Up against impasse in our work, we often simply try harder in the hope that if we finally do enough, we will eventually break through.

Impasse is announcing to me that something profound is changing, has changed, and we are struggling to catch up with that change. Something new is occurring in our world, in our human history, to which we are struggling to respond, with our efforts still falling short. It is demanding of us that we change how we think and move through this world.

> In going into the impasse rather than trying to avoid it, I found it not dead or empty but vivid and vibrant and terrible.

This will require an intense *listening* to the signs of the times, *listening* to what is happening. In order to listen, we have to become quiet, and we have to find the places/spaces where the "noise" of the world and of our cluttered lives is silenced.

In this circle of contemplation, we listened not only to what is speaking in our own hearts about impasse and its meaning, but in the hearts of others. We heard our voices, our feelings, our insights, our wisdom reflected back to us in ways that gave them more vivid life, richness, and depth. We learned from one another—not only in the words we spoke, but also in our shared silence, our quiet yoga meditation, the shared light of our candles, our bread breaking, our laughter, song, and dance. Each of these moments opened for me a space where I could "come out" and

145

be held in gentleness, joy, appreciation, and friendship. It was all okay, all okay.

In that shared space of impasse held lovingly opened by a circle of contemplation, I began to appreciate just how profound, radical, and fundamental a transformation is taking place inside my soul after more than two decades of looking the violence of our world squarely in the face. I have stood over the Ground Zero of war zones and marginal communities in Central America—as twenty years after beginning this work I would stare into the Ground Zero of lower Manhattan ten days after the horror of 9/11, and many days in the months following. I have no answers for all of that suffering; no answers adequate to the terrible awe instilled by the violence.

OUTGROWING OLD ALLEGIANCES AND BELIEF STRUCTURES

What is the transformation? A loss of innocence, sure. Shattered hopes, yes. A "crisis" of faith, absolutely. But not as if one could go back to the old faith that is no longer adequate for the times in which we live. Rather, what emerged in that circle was this awareness that we are rapidly outgrowing old allegiances and belief structures, that it's not about changing or reforming existing unjust structures that hold us and so many others bound; it is about moving beyond them, shaking the dust from our feet, not waiting for them any longer. They cannot contain what this impasse is telling us, and in reality the effort to salvage them is very much part of the impasse experience.

146

There is this other conceit that many activists struggle with, one that goes back centuries to the dawn of the Age of Enlightenment, like the mechanistic physics that no longer speaks the reality of our cosmos—the belief that *this* action will have *this* result, or even more to the point, that we can control the result. Why should we not be able to when what we are working for is justice and respect for the dignity and rights of the human person?

In our circle of contemplation, what was said, felt, sung, danced, and brought to quiet prayer was the inescapable nature of the changes required of us if we are to greet this new moment in human history when so much that we have known is dying, so many old understandings, and so many institutions built upon those old understandings.

As we moved through this process of communal contemplation and dialogue, I found myself brought face-to-face with an inescapable-ness, the inevitability of the death of the old and the need to engage, with courage, the fear that comes from knowing we are no longer on sure ground.

I also felt the resistance. We live in impasse, we also construct it—when we are unable to move out of that which no longer works, when we prop it up, hold it up, even when it is failing. I felt the resistance, and the reluctance—because I know what it will mean in my life. I have a sense of the changes required, what letting-go will really mean.

In the safe space of the community, letting-go seemed possible. In that circle, we held each other in our fears, our longings, and said, here, in this space, go ahead and jump. We will be there for you.

And I discovered in that experience the potential we have—in community—to let go. What happened for me in this process of communal contemplation and dialogue was that I found within it a possibility for another way of journeying through this troubling, fearful time in our world. Moving in and out of solitary and communal reflection, engaging a dialogue rooted in an intense listening to the heart and soul of each other, hearing not only with the ear, but with the heart, the truth of the other—in a space where there is no judgment, sharing moments of vulnerability—this process provided a space in which to build the trusting beloved community. It is a place where what we struggle with can be brought forward, take on flesh, teach us, and invite us to be courageous in facing the unknown, the uncertain, the new.

In our circle, we began to touch the enormity of the changes that are occurring in our world and in our consciousness as a result of our increasing global awareness, our appreciation for the interconnectedness of our lives—rich and poor, producers and consumers—awakening to the limits of Earth's natural resources and the non-sustainability of our lifestyles. And it is scary and wonderful. Engaging impasse through communal contemplation and dialogue invited me to move into the deeper learning and wisdom of these years of solidarity work, to have the courage to face all of it, all of it. Alone, it has been at times overwhelming. In community, I found courage and company. It serves as a reminder that the human being is created for connection, for relationship, not for isolation.

It is easier to enter into the fear, doubt, and uncertainty in the company of others. We are not intended to do it alone. There is a listening that must occur, to know what life is teaching us in *this* moment, out of *this* experience. I believe that is the only way we move out of impasse—not by fighting it (which only strengthens it), but by engaging it in the quiet spaces of our spirits, in the company of friends.

Impasse Rich with Promise

And from that company, that space, we take this challenge with us: How can we be faithful to what was opened in these circles gatherings? How do we live truthfully, honestly, all that was shared here, in a world still so resistant to the upheaval of the old forms and structures that impasse has announced?

In our circle, we reflected on that darkest time of night before the first light of day. This was one way we described impasse. And we reflected that perhaps this impasse is our horizon—the horizon just before dawn. In that sense, it is rich with promise.

Margaret Swedish was executive director of the Religious Task Force on Central America and Mexico, from 1981 to 2004. Her first book, Like Grains of Wheat, co-authored with Marie Dennis, and published by Orbis Press, is based on the input and reflections of more than 230 U.S. Americans engaged in Central America solidarity work over the past twenty-five years.

Reflection Questions

As you read CRUCIBLE FOR CHANGE, you are invited to enter into your own sacred space. Let the energy of that sacred space guide your reflection.

1. In her introduction, Nancy Sylvester, IHM sets the context that led to the creation of the *Engaging Impasse* project. She states that we live at a crossroads of history and time in which we face extraordinary challenges. We are experiencing major shifts in consciousness that are reshaping our worldviews. How do these challenges affect your own life and work?

Identify the times you felt as though you were standing at the foot of the wall with the Humpty-Dumpty pieces of shattered ecclesial hopes and dashed dreams of social justice scattered around you.

Impasse is described in various ways in the stories. How would you describe impasse in your own work in ecclesial and/or societal arenas?

2. As Mary McCann, IHM relates in her outline of the *Engaging Impasse* process, circle participants shared their impasse stories in a communal setting of contemplative inquiry. Each woman, however, found the very act of writing her story a powerful experience. You may find writing your own story to be a powerful experience in your personal reflection on impasse. As you write, pay attention to the story's details, the feelings it evokes, the effect it has on you. It may be possible for you to share your story with an understanding friend—who perhaps will tell you her story. Take time to listen; pause after the story's telling. Ask questions for clarification. Respond to each other lovingly.

You may wish to use the visual arts, music, dance, or yoga to express the feelings evoked.

3. For Patricia Bruno, OP "engaging impasse meant I had to first acknowledge it, and indeed unearth some of my dormant understandings and intentionally buried feelings."

In engaging impasse, we found that it is probably most difficult to acknowledge our own complicity in our experiences of impasse. Doing so has the potential to take us to places that scare us—places where emotions run deep. Participants found it helpful to stay with those emotions, asking themselves in various ways why those emotions scared them so.

When you consider engaging impasse, are there places that scare you? How do you feel about that? Why do you feel that way?

4. Simone Campbell, SSS found that the "process of engagement of impasse means we do not have a clue about the results." Like others across the circles, Simone came to understand that transformation might just require "surrendering my Grand Plan."

What is your "Grand Plan"? Would you find it possible to give it up? What would help you?

5. In taking a loving look at the real, Pat Kozak, CSJ sees us standing "at the borders of...collapsing and dying systems." Our mission, she believes, is to "simply be present there without confrontation or animosity or fear."

Where do you find collapsing systems in your life and work? When you stand at the borders of dying systems, whom do you find standing with you? For whom or what are you grieving? How do you identify the hope you find there?

6. "Like rain on dry land," and in the company of one another, the activists in Mary Hunt's circle received the gift of knowing that they did not have to confront every instance of impasse head on. They could engage in nonviolent, life-affirming ways; they could do nothing more than pray.

What is the gift of rain for which your own dry land is thirsting?

7. Joellen McCarthy, Mary Ann Zollmann, and Peggy Nolan came to the *Engaging Impasse* circles as members of the BVM Leadership Team. From the experiences of sharing and solidarity, contemplation and dialogue they took with them "fresh courage to cross the threshold into a brand new day." In sharing and applying their experience to a particular situation concerning the celebration of Eucharist in their congregation, they recognized a new "power of the imagination to move [the congregation] to new places [that] we encouraged one another to imagine."

Imagine a world (or a situation in your life/work) that might be transformed by opening a space for communal contemplation and dialogue. What does it look and feel like?

8. Margaret Galiardi, OP and Rose Mary Meyer, BVM reflect on impasse through the lens of the new cosmology. What role does the new cosmology play in your own spirituality? What effect has it had in your life? Rose Mary has come to "an understanding of impasse as birthing creativity....Such engagement calls me to touch into bodymindspirit or Cosmos." When you ponder your own experience of impasse within the larger Universe Story what new possibilities do you intuit?

9. In her own engagement with impasse, Margaret Swedish sees change occurring in our world as it struggles to be something new, requiring of us "an intense listening."

Do you sense the changes? What is that something new in the universe that you sense? How do you see it finding expression in your own milieu? When you *listen*, what are you hearing?

Elinor Shea, OSU realized that participation in the circle process had radically transformed her impasse. She had arrived at a moment of "a new naming, a new energy, a new hope." We hope your reading of the stories shared in Crucible for Change and your reflections on these questions have hinted at a new energy, a new hope to be discovered by engaging impasse through communal contemplation and dialogue. To learn more about the Institute for Communal Contemplation and Dialogue and this project, as well as opportunities to participate in new *Engaging Impasse* circles and related activities, please visit our website at www.engagingimpasse.org.

Endnotes

[1] The phrase "to take a long loving look at the real" to describe contemplation is popularly ascribed to the English mystics of the Middle Ages. Wayne Teasdale, A MONK IN THE WORLD (Novato, California: New World Library, 2002), p. 23.

[2] To read more extensively about these influences, please go to the project's website: www.engagingimpasse.org

[3] Although there are many sources for explaining the world-view ushered in by the Enlightenment, I drew significantly from WHO'S AFRAID OF SCHRODINGER'S CAT? by Ian Marshall and Danah Zohar (New York: Quill, 1997), pp. xix-xxv.

[4] *Ibid.*, pp. xxv-xxvii.

[5] Timothy Ferris, COMING OF AGE IN THE MILKY WAY (New York: William Morrow and Company, Inc., 1988), p. 208.

[6] *Ibid.*, p. 205.

[7] *Ibid.*

[8] Sidney Liebes, Elisabet Sahtouris, and Brian Swimme, A WALK THROUGH TIME (New York: Wileny and Sons, 1998), p. 8.

[9] *Ibid.*, p. 24.

[10] JUSTICE IN THE WORLD, Synod of Bishops, Second Annual Assembly, 1971, Article 6.

[11] Constance FitzGerald, OCD, "Impasse and Dark Night," WOMEN'S SPIRITUALITY RESOURCES FOR CHRISTIAN DEVELOPMENT, ed. Joann Wolski Conn, (New York: Paulist Press, 1986), p. 299-301.

[12] Richard Falk develops the emancipatory perspectives in major religions that are necessary to address the critical issues that confront us as a planet in his book, RELIGION AND HUMANE GLOBAL GOVERNANCE (New York: Palgrave, 2001). These emancipatory perspectives include reaffirmation of the sacred, embrace of human solidarity, and recognition that spiritual longing can take many authentic forms.

[13] FitzGerald, p. 299.

[14] JUSTICE IN THE WORLD.

[15] For the full LCWR Address, "Everything Before Us Brought Us to This Moment!" go to www.engagingimpasse.org and click on "Impasse," where you will find an imbedded link to the address.

[16] Amy McFrederick, OP, "Into Darkness and Impasse," Dominican Sisters, Great Bend, Kansas, 2002.

[17] Laura Swan, THE FORGOTTEN DESERT MOTHERS (New York/Mahwah, N.J.: Paulist Press, 2002), p. 47.

[18] At the end of the yearlong process, each participant received a small vigil light holder with an image sketched in dark blue glass of a Native American petroglyph, named *She Who Watches*. It was a replica of the image on the bowl, described on p. xiii, which featured so significantly in our gatherings.

[19] RILKE'S BOOK OF HOURS: LOVE POEMS TO GOD, trans. by Anita Burrows and Joanna Macy (New York: Riverhead Books, 1996), p. 57.

[20] THE ESSENTIAL RUMI, trans. by Coleman Banks and John Moyle (San Francisco: HarperCollins, 1997), p. 36.

[21] BREAKTHROUGH: MEISTER ECKHART'S CREATION SPIRITUALITY IN NEW TRANSLATION, Introduction and Commentary by Matthew Fox (Garden City, N.Y: Image Books, 1980), p. 5.

[22] Nancy Sylvester, IHM, "Everything Before Us Brought Us to This Moment," Presidential Address to the Leadership Conference of Women Religious, Albuquerque, New Mexico, August 2000.

[23] "Clergy Clinic in Family Emotional Process," Lombard Mennonite Peace Center, facilitated by Richard Blackburn and Robert Williamson. We participated in this clinic one day a month, from August 2000 to May 2001.

[24] New Ways Ministry was founded in 1977 to provide "a gay-positive ministry of advocacy and justice for lesbian and gay Catholics and reconciliation within the larger Christian and civil communities."

[25] Mahatma K. Gandhi, as quoted on the MK Gandhi Institute for Nonviolence website, www.gandhiinstitute.org.

[26] Gerald May, WILL AND SPIRIT (New York: Harper Collins Publishers, 1982), was a key resource during the Zen residency.

[27] Bodhisattva's Vow states this reality, in part: "we can be especially sympathetic and affectionate with foolish people, particularly with someone who...persecutes us with abusive language. That very abuse conveys the Buddha's boundless loving-kindness. It is a compassionate device to liberate us entirely from the mean-spirited delusions we have built up with our wrongful conduct from the beginningless past." From the teachings, or *Sutras*, of the Diamond *Sangha*, or a group of Buddhist commu-

nities sharing the common founder Aiken Roshi (see http://www.diamondsangha.org).

[28] See Matthew 17 and Mark 9.

[29] See the poem by Scott Cairns, "The Entrance of Sin," RECOVERED BODY (New York: George Braziller Publisher, 1998).

[30] FitzGerald, p. 299.

[31] *Ibid.*, p. 308.

[32] FitzGerald, "A Discipleship of Equals: Voices from the Tradition—Teresa of Avila and John of the Cross," A DISCIPLESHIP OF EQUALS: THEOLOGY INSTITUTE PUBLICATIONS, ed. Francis A. Eigo (Villanova, Pennsylvania: The Villanova University Press, 1988), p. 87.

[33] Albert Einstein in Peter Russell, THE WHITE HOLE IN TIME (San Francisco: Harper, 1992), p. 80.

[34] Thomas Berry, THE GREAT WORK (New York: Bell Tower, 1999), p.10.

[35] Barbara Marx Hubbard, CONSCIOUS EVOLUTION: AWAKENING THE POWER OF OUR SOCIAL POTENTIAL (California: New World Library, 1998), p.25.

[36] Mary Conrow Coelho, AWAKENING UNIVERSE, EMERGING PERSONHOOD:THE POWER OF CONTEMPLATION IN AN EVOLVING UNIVERSE (Ohio: Wyndham Hall Press, 2002), p. 110.

[37] Berry, "The Determining Features of the Ecozoic Era," Unpublished Notes.

[38] John of the Cross, "Living Flame of Love" in THE COLLECTED WORKS OF JOHN OF THE CROSS, ed. Kieran Kavanaugh, OCD and Otilio Rodríguez, OCD (Washington, D.C: Institute of Carmelite Studies, 1979), p. 718.

[39] Paulo Coelho, THE ILLUSTRATED ALCHEMIST: A FABLE ABOUT FOLLOWING YOUR DREAM, trans. Alan R. Clarke, illustrations by Moebius (New York: HarperCollins Books, 1993), p. 30.

[40] FitzGerald, "Impasse and Dark Night" in LIVING WITH APOCALYPSE: SPIRITUAL RESOURCES FOR SOCIAL COMPASSION (New York: Harper & Row, 1984).

[41] Elinor Shea, OSU, "Spiritual Direction and Social Consciousness," THE WAY SUPPLEMENT 54 (Autumn 1985), pp. 30-42.

[42] Pema Chodron, THE WISDOM OF NO ESCAPE AND THE PATH OF LOVING KINDNESS (Boston & London: Shambhala Publications, 2001) pp. 56-64.

[43] McFrederick.

[44] Pema Chodron, THE PLACES THAT SCARE YOU: A GUIDE TO FEARLESSNESS, narr. Tami Simon, audiocassette (Louisville, Colorado: Sounds True, 2001).

[45] Denise Levertov, "Primary Wonder" in THE STREAM AND THE SAPPHIRE (New York: New Directions, 1997), p. 33.

[46] Karl Rahner, EXPERIENCE OF SELF AND EXPERIENCE OF GOD THEOLOGICAL INVESTIGATIONS, Vol.XIII (New York: Crossroad, 1983), pp. 122-132.

[47] McFrederick.

[48] St. John of the Cross, DARK NIGHT OF THE SOUL, trans. Mirabai Starr (New York: Riverhead Books, 2002).

[49] Drawing on the lines from T.S. Eliot, FOUR QUARTETS (New York: Harvest Books, 1968), on p. 59., "We shall not cease from exploration/And the end of all our exploring/Will be to arrive where we started/And know the place for the first time."

[50] JUSTICE IN THE WORLD.

[51] Adrienne Rich, "Natural Resources" in THE FACT OF A DOORFRAME: SELECTED POEMS 1950-2001 (New York: W.W. Norton & Company, 2002), p. 167.

[52] Oscar Romero, comment to journalist, February 1980.

[53] See *She Who Watches*, p. xiii.

About the Editors

Nancy Sylvester, IHM is the Founder and President of the Institute for Communal Contemplation and Dialogue. She also serves as Executive Director of the Institute's first major project, *Engaging Impasse: Circles of Contemplation and Dialogue*. In 2001, Nancy completed a three-year term in the Presidency of the Leadership Conference of Women Religious, which overlapped in part her six-year service as vice president of her religious

 congregation, the Sisters, Servants of the Immaculate Heart of Mary, Monroe, Michigan. Prior to this, Nancy served on the staff of NET-WORK, a national Catholic social justice lobby, from 1977 through 1992, and as National Coordinator for the last ten of those years. Nancy loves to dance, sing show tunes, and read mysteries. She enjoys being by the water and walking in nature.

Mary Jo Klick is Project Coordinator of the Engaging Impasse project. She serves as a consultant with the United States Catholic Mission Association and the Catholic Mission Forum, planning Mission Congress 2005. As a consultant with the National Black Sisters' Conference, Mary Jo was Coordinator of the first National Gathering for Black Catholic Women in 2001. She was on the staff of NET-WORK, a national Catholic social justice lobby, from 1983 to 1993. Mary Jo enjoys spending time with family and friends. She is an avid  reader and collector of women's biographies and hopes to contribute to the genre in the future. Mary Jo loves poetry and writing haiku, sculpture and sculpting in clay, walking in nature, especially in the lush mountains of the eastern United States, and entering the enchanted landscape of New Mexico where she believes her spirit resides.

Institute for Communal Contemplation and Dialogue

Engaging Impasse: Circles of Contemplation and Dialogue is a project of the Institute for Communal Contemplation and Dialogue. Founded in 2002, the Institute is a tax-exempt charitable and religious organization. Its purpose is to resource, educate, and organize people of faith to reflect, analyze, and act on critical issues facing Church and society through a process of communal contemplation and dialogue.

The Institute is under the auspices of the Sisters, Servants of the Immaculate Heart of Mary, Monroe, Michigan. Its Board of Directors includes Dorothy Ettling, CCVI; Jane Herb, IHM; Mary Jo Klick; Bette Moslander, CSJ; and Nancy Sylvester, IHM. Julia Darlow serves as legal counsel and Margaret Alandt, IHM as financial administrator.

We invite you to visit www.engagingimpasse.org, where you will find reflective articles on dialogue, contemplation, impasse, globalization, the new cosmology, and shifting worldviews in societal and ecclesial contexts. The website also provides information about future activities of the Institute.

Institute for Communal Contemplation and Dialogue
8531 West McNichols
Detroit, Michigan 48221
(313) 341-7208
circles@engagingimpasse.org